STEVE

MY M

ITALIAN

MY FATHER'S

JEWISH

& I'M IN THERAPY

COOKBOOK

The two most important influences in Italian & Jewish families are:

#1. The Family #2. The Food...

Wait....maybe...

#1. Food #2. Family

This wonderful book blends into a medley of classic Italian and Jewish recipes with Steve's hilarious stories folded in for flavor.

Enjoy!

Compiled Tested Edited

Jane Evers

Stillwater Media, Inc.

Boynton Beach, Florida

www.stevesolomon.net

SECOND EDITION

Compiled * Tested * Edited by Jane Evers

Library of Congress Cataloging-in-Publication

My Mother's Italian, My Father's Jewish and I'm in Therapy &

Home for the Holidays Cookbook

ISBN 978-0-9728378-1-1

Table of Contents

MY MOTHER'S ITALIAN RECIPES

Soups...

It ain't just Minestrone anymore

Main Entrees...

and the winner is...

You worked hard, you deserve this. OR Hope you saved some room OR By now you'll need a doggy-bag (ta-go box)

Pasta & Risotto...
"spaghetti" never looked so good

Vegetables...
these "sides" should be in the front

Desserts...
did you eat all your veggies? (sides?)

MY FATHER'S JEWISH RECIPES

Soups...

You'll never miss Campbell's again

Entrees...

Let the games begin...

Who wants seconds... ok, thirds? Fourths?

Vegetables...

even baby cousin Moisha's gonna love these... and he hates everything!

Starches...
these carbs are allowed

Desserts...
did you call your mother today? Ok, you can have dessert!

From Steve...

What better way to get to know my crazy family: You can always find us around a kitchen or dining room table. My Mom, Grandma Angelina, Bubbie, all my Aunts even some of my Uncles had their signature dish.

Since writing "My Mother's Italian, My Father's Jewish and I'm in Therapy"—now one of the longest one-man comedies in history, I've realized how much food has been a happy part of my life - especially during the holidays. I've asked my family and friends to contribute to this cookbook. Some recipes have been in my family for years others are fairly new. Most have been adjusted and tested by Jane for simplicity in cooking and, despite my objections, tailored towards healthy eating.

You will find no schmaltz (chicken fat) or heavy oils. There is limited sugar and less salt than the normal Jewish or Italian recipe. Jane's adapted the recipes to help keep our cholesterol and sugar levels in balance. You might still get heartburn, but only from aggravation.

I know many of my relatives would not approve of these changes, but new dietary guidelines and our healthier living styles make these changes necessary – Momma already filed a suit against Jane for changing Momma's recipes! At least, by following these recipes, your indigestion and gastric reflux will be under control.

In any event, the recipes are authentic and the stories true and hysterical. All these dishes have been developed with love of tradition and are really very delicious. So, my friends, enjoy, essen, manga....

From Jane (Steve's life partner & author of this cookbook)...

This book was first written for the Broadway opening of "My Mother's Italian, My Father's Jewish & I'm in Therapy", in November, 2006. The show ran in New York for almost two years. It's now one of the longest running one-man-shows in Broadway history.

Since Broadway, Steve went back on the road. He's spent his spare time writing two more shows; "My Mother's Italian, My Father's Jewish & I'm **Still** in Therapy", in 2008 and "My Mother's Italian, My Father's Jewish & I'm Home for the Holidays" in 2010.

In 2009, an International Production Company started touring the first show, "My Mother's Italian, My Father's Jewish & I'm in Therapy" in South Africa. Canada, Great Britain, New Zealand and Australia are being scheduled as this revised cookbook is being printed.

Also in 2009, a national touring company began producing "My Mother's Italian, My Father's Jewish & I'm in Therapy." The touring company uses other actors/comedians and has played in Phoenix, AZ, Philadelphia, PA Columbus, OH, San Diego, CA & Toronto, Canada. Many more venues are being planned for the 2013 – 2014 Season. Check the website, www.stevesolomon.net for the current schedule.

Steve is now working on an audio book about his hilarious life adventures and he just completed the CD of "...Home for the Holidays." Look for it at the shows and on his website.

Thanks to all of Steve's wonderful fans. Without your support and heartfelt enthusiasm, Steve's shows would never be so successful. He appreciates each and every one of you.

Our journey continues... Just remember that when you follow your heart, at any age, your dreams can come true.

Foreword

When my Grandma Angelina and my Momma got into the kitchen to start cooking for a holiday it was like watching a SWAT team preparing for an assault. Dad and Uncle Paulie ("the mental midget" as momma called him) would return from the grocer, we didn't have supermarkets per se back then, with the ammunition; fresh everything.

My cousin and I would stand close by the kitchen, like seagulls hovering over a picnic, waiting for scraps. I never remembered either my Momma or Grandma referring to a recipe.

They had unusual words for measuring purposes. They used words like: pinch, schkootch, smidge, a lilla more. Measuring ingredients was more of an art rather than a science; taste and color and textures determined need. Too much salt? Throw in a potato. Too bitter? Pour in sugar (and I do mean pour) Too dark? Add water. And, amazingly enough, the final product was always the same as when they cooked it 25 years ago. Well... in truth, if it tasted different, no one had the balls to mention it to Grandma. It amazed me that Uncle Paulie, 325 pounds, 5'8 inches tall (Grandma was 4'7") could lift a car to change its tire, had to shave three times a day...... but would cry if Grandma yelled at him. "PAULIE!!!!" everybody got quiet.

I remember the time Uncle Paulie was almost vanquished from the family when he committed one of the worst acts of terrorism anyone could do against an Italian family....Grandma found a jar of Chef Boyardee in his fridge. He's still going to confession about it.

Her best food quote? I asked Grandma why Italians eat snails. She looked up from the spaghetti steam...." They don't like fast food!"

Acknowledgements

Thanks to everyone in back of the scenes and in front of the house who have made this exciting adventure so successful. Since the first printing in 2006, many changes have taken place in our family. We sadly lost Steve's & my Mom as well as Steve's sister, the smoker, Shelly. It was wonderful that they were able to experience the success of the Broadway show. We miss them every day, but acknowledge their memory with much love.

Some basic items needed in an Italian Kitchen

Canned tomatoes: Diced, crushed, whole plum, sauce, paste. Have a variety of can sizes

Cheese: Parmesan, mozzarella, ricotta, mascarpone

Seasonings: Oregano, basil, thyme, parsley (fresh or dried), capers, saffron, anchovies, bay leaf, rosemary

Nuts: Pine, almond

Wine: Marsala, Madiera, Brandy

Vinegar: Balsamic, white wine, red wine

Soups: Chicken, vegetable, beef broth

Vegetables: Spinach, zucchini, eggplant, carrots, onions, garlic, celery, olives, dried porcini mushrooms, chili peppers

Oils: Olive, vegetable

Pasta: Variety

Ask a real Italian about their sauce and they know you're NO Italian. Real Italians call it *gravy*. If I called it sauce in front of Grandma Angelina, she'd say I was hanging out with a bad crowd. I also learned that oregano, the staple spice in every Italian house, adds aroma rather than taste. Grandma taught me lots of great kitchen tidbits. I did have one problem; I hated garlic. My Mom and Grandma found out one day while they watched me pick garlic pieces out of the sauce....sorry, gravy. Grandma went berserk. "Stoonahd! ....Doena you know Garlic isa good for you. Garlic, she makes a you bloodpressa ho-kay...How my gonna teacha you.....you so stubborn....Eata right and dat means plenty garlic...ana you live long!. "But Grandma", I said,....."You told me Grandpa Mario died when he was only 48......" She made a face, growled, bit her finger grabbed the wooden spoon and I suddenly remembered I had to clean out my sock drawer immediately.

Later, I walked into Grandma's kitchen and watched her on a rickety chair with a mop in her hand, washing the ceiling. The ceiling? I later came to realize that Italians, all Italians, talk with their hands..... even when they're holding a wooden spoon covered with spaghetti sauce...I mean gravy.

MY MOTHER'S ITALIAN RECIPES

ITALIAN SOUPS

It ain't just Minestrone anymore

Chilled Tomato Soup with Zucchini & Ricotta

Italian Bean & Sausage Soup

Lentil Soup with Escarole & Pancetta

Stracciatella

Italian Bread

Fresh toasted garlic bread, smothered in fresh butter, crunchy, just out of the oven. It was a meal in itself. When Momma brought out that basket of joy and placed it on the table, everyone dove for the first piece. There was never enough because you couldn't stop. On a good day, Momma made four gigantic toasted Italian garlic breads. By the end of the meal, there wasn't a morsel left. It doesn't get "breader" than this.

Chilled Tomato Soup with Zucchini and Ricotta

Stove top cooking

Serves 4

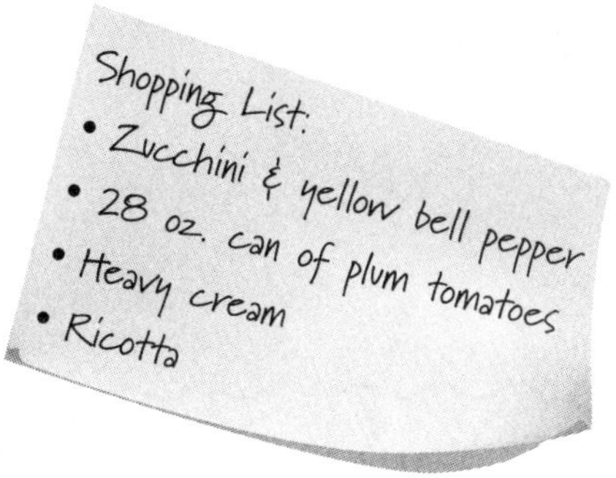

Ingredients

1 zucchini, peeled & cubed

2 tablespoons extra-virgin olive oil, divided, plus a little extra

1- 32 ounce can whole plum tomatoes

10 slices Cuban or Italian bread, crusts removed, cubed

salt and freshly ground pepper

¼ cup heavy cream

8 ounces fresh ricotta

julienne carrot & yellow bell peppers for garnish

1. Peel the zucchini. Julienne the peel, and reserve for garnish.
2. Cube peeled zucchini.
3. In a skillet over medium heat, warm 1 tablespoon of olive oil.
4. Add cubed zucchini to the skillet, and sauté for about 5 minutes (until soft). Remove from the heat, and set aside to cool.
5. Pour tomatoes and bread into a food processor. While processing, add the heavy cream in a slow, steady stream.
6. At this point, you can either serve the soup at room temperature or place tomato/bread soup in refrigerator to chill.
7. When ready to serve, distribute the sautéed zucchini among individual bowls, and pour the soup on top.
8. Place the ricotta in a bowl, and stir in 1 tablespoon of olive oil.
9. To serve, distribute the tomato soup among bowls. Use 2 spoons and place the ricotta into quenelles, and arrange on the surface of the soup.
10. Garnish with the julienne zucchini peel, carrot and yellow pepper, and drizzle with olive oil.

Bean and Sausage Soup

Talk about a hearty soup. Remember when they said if you eat that...."it'll put hair on your chest..." Well, my Uncle Paulie must have grown up on this soup. He's got a rug on his chest. One caveat... Lots of people, eating lots of this soup in a small room....need I go into details again? As Momma always said to me, "mangiate come una mucca." (you eat like a cow) I don't know what that has to do with Italian Bean and Sausage Soup. It just came to mind. Enjoy!

Italian Bean and Sausage Soup

Stove top cooking
Serves 6

Shopping List:
- Italian sweet sausage
- 28 oz. can plum tomatoes
- Medium pasta shells
- 19 oz. can cannelloni beans

Ingredients

12 oz. sweet Italian sausage
2 teaspoons olive oil
1 cup onion, chopped
2 teaspoons garlic, minced
1 can (28 oz.) whole plum tomatoes
3 ½ cups hot water
2 cups cooked medium pasta shells (4 oz.)
2 chicken bouillon cubes (or 2 teaspoons broth granules)
1 (19 oz.) can Cannelloni (white kidney beans) or other white beans

1. Remove sausage from casing. Crumble sausage into oil, stir in onions and garlic. Cook over high heat, stirring often until sausage browns and onion are soft.
2. Cut up tomatoes. Add tomatoes and the juice, water, pasta and bouillon cubes to pot.
3. Bring to a boil over high heat. Reduce heat. Cover and simmer 7 minutes.
4. Rinse and drain beans. Add to soup and simmer until pasta is tender.

Lentil Soup with Escarole and Pancetta

Stove top cooking

Serves 4 to 6

Shopping List:
- Pancetta
- Green lentils
- Canned chopped tomatoes
- Chicken or vegetable broth
- Escarole

Ingredients

2 tablespoons olive oil

4 slices of pancetta, finely chopped

1 small onion, finely chopped

2 cloves of garlic, minced

2 carrots, finely diced

2 stalks of celery, finely chopped

2 cups dry green lentils (See note 1)

1 cup, chopped canned tomatoes

1 bay leaf

1 ½ quarts(6 cups) chicken or vegetable broth or water or a combination (see note 2)

Salt & Pepper

1 teaspoon dried Italian seasoning mix

2 slices Italian bread cut Into 1 ½ Inch cubes with crusts removed

½ head escarole, washed, dried, and chopped

1 tablespoon balsamic vinegar

1. Heat the olive oil with the pancetta, and cook until it is no longer pink.
2. Add the onions, celery, carrots, and garlic over medium heat until they are tender.
3. Add the lentils, tomatoes, chicken broth, salt, pepper and bay leaf. Bring to a boil and then reduce the heat to a simmer. Continue to cook over low heat, adding water as needed until the lentils are tender but have retained their shape, (about 40 minutes).

4. Add the bread to the soup, and using a whisk, break up the bread to help thicken the soup.
5. Add the escarole and cook until tender, an additional 5 minutes.
6. Stir in the balsamic vinegar to mix.
7. Serve topped with a drizzle of olive oil and some grated parmesan cheese.

Note 1: Lentil soup can, at times, be either chewy, or mushy, but using the best lentils you can find will help. French green lentils or the simple larger, regular green ones work well.

Note 2: You can either use all water to make the soup, or chicken or vegetable broth which will make a richer tasting soup

Stracciatella

Stove top cooking
Serves 4

Ingredients

3 cups chicken broth
3 eggs
¼ cup fresh bread crumbs
¼ cup parmesan cheese
salt & pepper
4 tablespoons fresh, chopped parsley

1. In a saucepan, bring the broth to a boil.
2. In a bowl, beat together the eggs, bread crumbs and cheese. Add salt and pepper.
3. Remove the broth from the heat, and pour in the egg mixture, stirring constantly.
4. Pour the soup into four separate bowls, and sprinkle with the parsley, and additional cheese if desired.

Note: Pastina (small pasta) may also be added to this soup.

Tough act to follow

Having grown up in a home where eating took precedence over everything, I was rather dismayed when I found out that my new bride now my ex new bride, couldn't cook. That's not to say that she didn't try. Since Mama & Grandma had set culinary standards, they were a tough act to follow. My ex would try to replicate some of my family's secret recipes. The problem became apparent when, whatever she tried to make-- even if she followed the recipe exactly, it always came out like Vito's blue plate special at the Main Street Diner. Something was amiss. "She shouldn't be that bad?" I thought.

One day in the middle of the same argument that I've been having with my Mom about my ex, -- she would present me with a litany of reasons why she was no good for me, held me back financially and most of all, couldn't cook. I asked my Mother how come, if she follows your recipe exactly, everything taste like crap? My mother shouted, how should I know? She must be doing something wrong. Then I noticed that my Mom bit her lip. That was the flashing neon sign that said Mom was lying. Being an adult I wasn't too afraid that she would hit me for being precocious so, since she was a foot & a half shorter than me, I cornered her and questioned her. She confessed. Grandma & Mama used to leave out parts of recipes so no one could duplicate their masterpieces exactly. A pinch of salt became...add some salt. A teaspoon became a tablespoon. Blood IS thicker than water.

ITALIAN ENTREES

Hope you saved some room

"Skinny" Chicken Parmesan

Chicken Marsala

Italian Meatloaf

Italian Fish Stew

Chicken Cacciatore...
why the recipe is not in this cookbook...

Mom used to make this dish often. I really didn't like it; not because it didn't taste great... mom made it with whole chicken pieces... meat AND bones. And, since I was a "utensil-challenged" child; I ate the big pieces with my hands...And..., since Mom's Chicken Cacciatore was always smothered in Mom's special tomato sauce... Mr. Clean spray and Bounty was always handy. It was a bone chilling experience.

I developed the following recipe while on a very strict diet, but I wanted to have the taste of a parmesan meal. My aim was to cut as many calories as possible, but still keep the traditional flavors intact. Steve was very happy with the results.

"Skinny" Chicken Parmesan

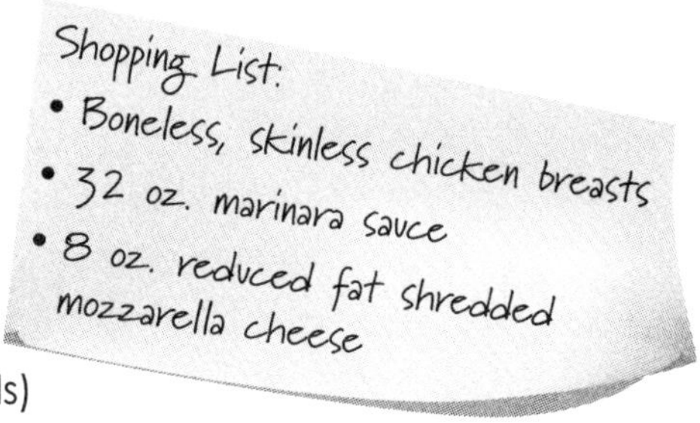

Grill or pan grill

Oven

Serves 4

Ingredients

4 skinless, boneless chicken breasts pounded very thin (about 1½ pounds)

Marinara Sauce "Gravy" (32 oz.)

8 oz reduced fat shredded mozzarella cheese

Non-stick oil

Parmesan cheese (garnish)

Marinade for chicken

1 cup of Grapefruit juice (or any citrus juice)

2 Tablespoons olive oil

Italian herbs to taste

Or substitute 1 cup of any type of Italian dressing that you like for olive oil & herbs

1. Make sure chicken breasts are thinly pounded.
2. Mix marinade and submerge breast for at least 8 hours – I make a double portion of chicken and eat the barbecued chicken one night and then make the parmesan chicken a couple of days later.
3. Grill on barbeque or in ridged grill pan on stove. Don't overcook.
4. Take a baking pan and spray with non-stick oil.
5. Lay a small amount of the Marinara sauce in the bottom of the pan.
6. Place the grilled chicken on top of sauce.
7. Add another tablespoon or two on each chicken breast.
8. Sprinkle with the mozzarella cheese.
9. Cover pan and bake in oven at 325 degrees for 20 minutes until cheese is melted.
10. Sprinkle with parmesan, if desired. Steve does not like parmesan so I leave that off his portion.

Chicken* Marsala

Stove top cooking

Serves 4

Shopping List:

- Boneless chicken breasts
- Fresh parsley
- Sliced mushrooms
- Marsala wine
- Balsamic vinegar

Ingredients

¼ cup all-purpose flour for coating (I use rice flour)

½ teaspoon salt

¼ teaspoon ground black pepper

*4 skinless, boneless chicken breast halves (about 6 oz each) - pounded ¼ inch thick

4 - 6 tablespoons olive oil

1 ½ cups sliced mushrooms (Crimini/Button/Portobello etc.)

½ & ¾ cups Marsala wine

¼ cup balsamic vinegar

¼ – ½ cup fresh parsley chopped

1. In a shallow dish or bowl, mix together the flour, salt, pepper.
2. Lightly coat chicken pieces in flour mixture.
3. In a large skillet, heat oil over medium-high heat. Place chicken in the pan, and lightly brown on both sides.
4. Take out chicken pieces and place on a plate. Add mushrooms to the pan and cook until limp (3 – 5 minutes). Flash with ½ cup wine.
5. Put chicken back in pan. Add another ¾ cup wine, balsamic vinegar and some salt & pepper. Lower heat.
6. Cover skillet; simmer chicken on low-medium heat for 15 minutes, turning once, until chicken is no longer pink and juices run clear.
7. Sprinkle with parsley.

***Note**: You can use chicken, veal even thinly sliced beef for this dish. Each portion should be between 4 – 6 ounces.

Italian Meat Loaf or Meat Balls

Oven at 350 degrees
Serves 8

Shopping List:
You should have everything in the house

Meat Loaf Ingredients

2 ½ pounds lean hamburger or chopped turkey or mixture of whatever meats you prefer

2 cups canned Diced Tomatoes

2 eggs, beaten

1 cup onion, finely chopped

2 cups Italian bread crumbs

¼ cup ketchup or chili sauce

1-2 tablespoons horseradish

1 tablespoon Dijon mustard

Spice Mix Ingredients

1 Teaspoon of each: Oregano, dry mustard, thyme, garlic powder, onion powder, basil and freshly ground black pepper.

Add 1 Tablespoon Kosher Salt. Mix it all together.

Dash or two of Tabasco (optional)

3 tablespoons Worcestershire sauce

Topping Ingredients

¼ cup reduced homemade tomato sauce*

¼ cup bottled grocery store chili sauce or ketchup

¼ cup brandy

⅓ cup cheddar cheese, (or any of your favorite Italian cheeses).

Mix the ketchup or chili sauce and tomato sauce. You'll sprinkle the cheese over the sauce.

***Note:** Put the tomato sauce in a sauce pan, add about 1 Tablespoon of lemon juice, 2 Tablespoon Worcestershire sauce, and about ¼ cup of brandy. Reduce this into a near paste, and you'll really intensify the flavor of the tomato sauce.

Preparation Of The Meat Loaf:

1. Preheat oven to 350 degrees.
2. Mix all of the ingredients, except the topping, in a large mixing bowl.
3. Then, place the mixture into a large bread pan and spread it evenly into a loaf.
4. Bake for about 1 hour. Drain off the excess liquid and "ice" it with the topping.
5. Bake about 15 more minutes, or until the cheese is toasted, and you'll be in for a gourmet treat.

Preparation of the Meat Balls:

Follow steps 1 & 2. Instead of putting in loaf pan, shape mixture into medium large balls. (Should make 16 – 20 balls). Place on cookie sheet and bake in oven about 25 - 30 minutes Don't use the topping on the meatballs unless they are very close together or the topping will burn.

Italian Fish Stew

Stove top
Serves 4

Ingredients

½ cup olive oil

3 cloves garlic, chopped

1 tablespoon basil

½ teaspoon red pepper flakes

½ cup dry white wine

1 28 oz. can Italian tomatoes (crushed or peeled or diced)

2 tablespoons tomato paste

8 oz. clam broth or clam juice

1 teaspoon salt or to taste

1 package frozen cod fillets (8 ounces or more – depending on how hungry you are)

1 package frozen haddock fillets (8 ounces or more – depending on how hungry you are)

1 pound frozen or fresh shrimp, shelled and deveined

You can use any other type of fish or seafood. I use clams, basa or any other sweet fish. Sometimes I add squid, calamari, mussels etc.

4 tablespoons ditali or other small pasta

2 tablespoons finely chopped parsley

Grated lemon rind

1. Heat oil in heavy kettle or Dutch oven and sauté garlic, basil and red pepper until tender.
2. Add wine and simmer about 5 minutes or until liquid is somewhat reduced.
3. Add tomatoes, tomato paste, clam broth and salt
4. Simmer, uncovered 20 to 30 minutes to thicken sauce.
5. Cut fish into large pieces and add fish and shrimp to sauce

6. Cover and simmer 10 minutes or until fish is just done (it will look opaque)
7. Remove fish to serving dish and keep warm
8. Add pasta to sauce, cover and simmer 10 minutes longer until pasta is tender
9. Pour over fish in serving dish
10. Garnish with parsley and grated lemon
11. Stew may be ladled over Italian bread or served over rice

Pasta - The staple of an Italian family. Al Dente... never undercooked. Italian logic. Eat five servings of vegetables a day; you lose weight and stay healthy. Pasta's made from wheat---wheat's a vegetable---you do the math! Big and tall shop here we come.

When I was growing up, we had spaghetti with...? It was spaghetti, just spaghetti. There was no Rigatoni, Fusilli, Penne, Ziti, Orzo,... Just plain old spaghetti. When did spaghetti become pasta? I think about the same time that Italian Restaurants became Risterantes. D'Italiano. Then a bowl of spaghetti became a bowl of pasta and the price went up accordingly.

Italian Pasta & Risotto

"Spagette" never looked so good

Pasta Variations on a Theme

Here's an idea that Jane uses all the time. She mixes & matches different pasta, with a sauce, and throws in either roasted veggies, meat, fish or poultry. The varieties are endless. Just look at some of the pasta choices available.

Tubular Pasta: Bocconcini, Bucatini, Calamarata (calamari), Canneroni, Cannelloni, Cannolicchi, , Cellentani, Chifferi, Chifferini, Elbow macaroni, Elicoidali, Fagioloni, , Garganelli, Gomiti, Macaroni, Maccheroni, Maccheroncelli, Magliette, Maltagliati, Manicotti, Mezzani Rigati, Mezze Penne, Mezzi Bombardoni, Mezzi Paccheri, Mezzi Rigatoni, Mostaccioli, Paccheri, Pasta al ceppo, Penne rigate, Penne Zita, Pennette, Pennine rigate, Pennoni, Perciatelli, Reginelle, Rigatoncini, Rigatoni, Sagne Incannulate, Spaccatelle, Trenne, Trennette, Tortiglioni, Tufoli, Ziti – Cut, Ziti – Long, Ziti rigati, Zitoni

Strand Pasta: Angel Hair (capelli d' angelo), Barbina, Bigoli, Capelli d'angelo (Angel Hair), Capellini, Chitarra (spaghetti alla chitarra), Ciriole, Fedelini (fidelini), Fusilli lunghi, Spaghetti, Spaghettini, Spaghettoni, Thin Spaghetti, Vermicelli

Ribbon Pasta Noodles: Bavette, Bavettine (mezze linguine), Fettuce, Fettuccine, Fettucelle, Kluski, Lasagne, Lasagnette, Lasagnotte, Linguettine, Linguine, Mafalde, Mafaldine, Pappardelle, Pillus, Pizzoccheri, Reginette, Riccia, Sagnarelli, Stringozzi, Tagliatelle, Taglierini (tagliolini, tonnarelli), Trenette (trinette), Tripoline

Stuffed Pasta: Agnolotti, Cappelletti (alpine hats), Cappelloni, Manti, Mezzaluna, Pansotti, Ravioli, Ravioloni, Ravioletti, Tortelli (anolini), Tortellini

Types of Sauces

There are literally hundreds of sauces, but many contain ingredients that Steve will not tolerate. In fact, his hatred of Parmesan cheese is a real hindrance in many of my recipes. Sometimes I make two sauces; one for him and one for me.

Aglio e olio - garlic, olive oil and parsley

Alfredo - butter, cream and freshly grated cheese served with fettuccine

Bolognese - rich meat sauce flavored with chicken livers, wine, vegetables and nutmeg. Served with butter and grated cheese; sometimes cream is added to the sauce. Also called ragu in parts of Italy other than Bologna

Burro - butter and grated Parmesan cheese

Funghi e piselli - sauce of mushrooms, bacon and fresh green peas

Marinara - sauce of fresh tomatoes, olive oil, garlic and basil

Pesto - grated cheese, pine nuts, basil and garlic pounded into a paste

Pomidoro - tomato sauce – simpler than marinara

Romana - meat and chicken sauce with chopped mushrooms

Vongole - clam sauce with onions, tomatoes, olive oil and garlic

Seth's Marinara Sauce (Gravy)

Stove top cooking
Makes loads of gravy

Shopping List:
- 2 cans of tomato sauce

Ingredients

1 large white or yellow onion, diced
1 large carrot, chopped, sautéed & pureed
2 tablespoons garlic, chopped
3 tablespoons extra virgin olive oil
2 teaspoons salt (or to taste)
2 teaspoons pepper (or to taste)
1 tablespoon dried oregano
1 tablespoon dried basil
1 tablespoon dried parsley
½ teaspoon crushed red pepper (or to taste)
1 cup wine (red wine)
2 large cans (28 ounces) of tomato sauce

1. Dice and chop up the onion and garlic.
2. Put pot on stove and add the extra virgin olive oil to the bottom of the pot, heat at medium high for a minute before adding onions and garlic. Cook onions and garlic till translucent and/or slightly golden brown.
3. Next add all your dried ingredients (salt, pepper, oregano, basil, parsley and crushed red pepper) and mix with spoon, lower heat a little bit. Cook until the oil, onions, garlic and dried ingredients look like a paste or for about 5-7 minutes.
4. Add 1 cup red wine and reduce to ½ cup liquid
5. Next add your tomato sauce and the carrot puree.
6. Lower heat to medium to medium low and let cook, while stirring occasionally. Adjust seasonings (salt & pepper).
7. Cook for a minimum of 1 hour and up to 6 hours in length.
8. Cool, then either store in refrigerator or use immediately.

Milanese Risotto

Shopping List:
- Arborio rice sometimes called Italian rice
- Fresh parsley
- Saffron threads

Stove top cooking
Serves 4 – 6

Ingredients

3 tablespoons olive oil
2 + 2 tablespoons butter
1 large onion, diced
¼ cup white wine
½ teaspoon saffron threads, (optional)
1 cup Arborio rice
5-8 cups vegetable/chicken/beef stock
½ cup Pecorino Romano cheese, shredded
¼ cup Italian Parsley, chopped, as garnish

1. Heat stock to slowly simmering in a sauce pan.
2. Heat a large, heavy skillet over medium heat. Add olive oil and 2 Tablespoons of butter.
3. When butter is just melted, add onions, stir to coat and sauté for 5 minutes. Add Arborio rice, stir to coat well, sprinkle in saffron threads.
4. Add wine and let absorb into rice.
5. Reduce heat to low and add enough stock to just cover the rice. As rice is uncovered, keep adding warm stock as needed to maintain covering. Continue this process for about 20 minutes, until rice is tender.
6. Allow last stock added to reduce until about 90 percent absorbed, then, add remaining 2 Tablespoons butter. Stir in well.
7. Add Pecorino Romano and stir it in well.
8. Remove from heat and let rest for 5 minutes while final liquid is absorbed. Your risotto Milanese should be rich and creamy. Rice should be tender.

This dish can be tailored to your specific needs. You can serve it as a side dish as written or you can add mushroom or peas when you sauté the onions for another type of side dish. Or, with the addition of grilled chicken or shrimp added to the top when finished, it can be a main dish.

Sausage and Wild Mushroom Risotto

Stove top cooking

Serves 4 main or 8 side

Shopping List:
- Italian sweet sausage
- Mushrooms – Portobello/shitake
- Madeira wine
- Chicken stock
- Aborio rice
- Asiago or Parmesan cheese

Ingredients

2 tablespoons olive oil

1 pound Italian sweet sausage

8 ounces Portobello mushrooms

10 ounces fresh shiitake mushrooms, stemmed, diced

1 teaspoon chopped fresh thyme

1 teaspoon chopped fresh oregano

1 ½ cups Madeira wine

6 cups chicken stock or canned low-salt chicken broth

½ cup (1 stick) butter

1 large onion, chopped

4 garlic cloves, minced

2 cups arborio rice or other medium-grain rice (about 13 ounces)

1 cup freshly grated Asiago/Parmesan cheese

1. Remove casings from sausage and crumble into ½-inch pieces
2. Stem & scrape dark gills from Portobello mushrooms, dice caps
3. Heat oil in large nonstick skillet over medium-high heat.
4. Add sausage and sauté until beginning to brown, about 3 minutes.
5. Add all mushrooms, thyme, and oregano and sauté until mushrooms are tender, about 10 minutes.
6. Add ½ cup Madeira; boil until almost absorbed, about 1 minute. Set aside.
7. Bring stock to simmer in large saucepan; remove from heat and cover to keep hot.
8. Melt butter in heavy large pot over medium-high heat. Add onion and garlic and sauté until onion is translucent, about 5 minutes.

9. Add rice; stir 2 minutes. Add remaining 1 cup Madeira; simmer until absorbed, about 2 minutes.
10. Add 1 cup hot stock; simmer until almost absorbed, stirring often, about 3 minutes. Continue to cook until rice is just tender and mixture is creamy, adding more stock by cupfuls, stirring often and allowing most stock to be absorbed before adding more, about 25 minutes.
11. Stir in sausage mixture. Season to taste with salt and pepper.
12. Transfer to serving bowl. Pass cheese separately.

Nonna's Lasagna

You know that old adage: There's always room for Jello?" There's always room for Grandma's Lasagna..... there better be. It was a miracle, a medley of flavors.. I liked the meat lasagna the best. One never knew just what meat it was and one never asked. "Meat's meat!" She would say. I'm convinced it was usually yesterday's meat smothered in things that covered up any semblance of recognition. Veal? Pork? Kidneys? Who cared? It was always good, really good but you had to make room cause you never said no to Grandma's lasagna. And thanks to Grandma's food mandates; we had nine bulimics in the family. Coincidence? I think not!

Simply Lasagna

Stove top cooking & oven at 375 degrees
Serves 8

Shopping List:
- Ground beef, turkey, chicken, veal, pork or combination.
- Ricotta & Mozzarella cheese
- Lasagna noodles
- Green pepper, onion
- Can of tomato sauce, tomato paste, sewed tomatoes
- Fresh parsley

Ingredients

1 lb lean ground beef/turkey/pork

½ 28 oz can or a (16 oz) stewed tomatoes

2 tablespoons olive oil

½ 6 oz can (3 oz) tomato paste

½ medium sweet white onion, diced

1 lb Ricotta cheese

½ large green bell pepper, diced

1 ½ lbs Mozzarella (large flat square slices)

1 lb dry lasagna noodles

¾ lb freshly grated parmesan cheese

¼ cup sugar

Garlic Powder, Oregano, Italian Spice, Salt

1 28 oz can tomato sauce

Garlic Salt, Parsley diced (fresh flat)

1 garlic clove, minced

White wine vinegar

The instructions are on the next page...

Simply Lasagna Instructions

1. Spray skillet with cooking spray
2. Brown lean ground beef in skillet until lightly browned and cooked through. Remove and drain. Dispose of excess fat & wipe pan.
3. In same pan, add diced green pepper and onion to skillet. Brown for a few minutes on medium high heat, add browned beef back in the skillet, lower the heat to low and continue to cook for 5 more minutes stirring frequently.
4. Transfer browned beef, green pepper and onions to 3 quart pot. Add tomato sauce & tomato paste. Open stewed tomatoes and dice, then add 2 teaspoons each of oregano, parsley, Italian spice. Add garlic and a pinch of garlic salt, to taste. Add a dash of white wine vinegar. Add sugar a couple tablespoons at a time, until desired level of sweetness, no more than ¼ cup of sugar.
5. Stir and allow sauce to simmer 15-45 minutes to thicken (do not scorch bottom, stir frequently). Remove from heat.
6. Cook 1 lb lasagna noodles in 6 quart pot to al dente. (Note noodles may be cooked in advance.) Stir often to prevent from sticking, use low boil. Add 1 Tablespoon oil & ½ teaspoon salt (if desired) to water. Drain in colander and place in cool water filled pan to keep from drying out and sticking together.
7. In dry lasagna pan, ladle one cup of sauce and spread along the bottom of the pan. Apply a layer noodles 3 length wise (edges overlapping). Ladle in sauce sparingly into center trough of 3 noodles. Apply a layer of mozzarella cheese slices on top of lasagna sauce. Place ricotta cheese dollops (about a Tablespoon) every 2 inches in center of noodles on top of mozzarella cheese slices, sprinkle grated parmesan cheese in thin even layer on top of ricotta cheese.
8. Apply second layer of noodles going in the opposite direction. Repeat three times topping with noodles. If you have extra sauce and cheese you can spread that over the top. Tent lasagna pan with aluminum foil (not touching noodles or sauce). Bake at 350 degrees until brown and bubbly. Allow to cool before serving.

What does she want?

Mom had strange ways of getting what she wanted. Sometimes I had to translate from momma to English. A poor translation on my part usually resulted in pain and suffering for me....case in point.

I'm sitting on the porch, reading a comic book; mom's sitting next to me and knitting names into a sweater..... think "Dickens." Mom looks up, "You feel like an apple?" "No thanks mom." I answered. She continued, "I just-a bought fresh sweet apples, the kind-a you like." I looked up from the comic, "No, I'm good, I don't want one." Mom's nostrils started to flare, "Ow come, every time I buy you exactly want you want, you don't eat it. So you know what? Let them rot in the fridge. I'll just throw them out, waste Daddy's money, because you decide that you don't want exactly what I buy for you...I can't believe it...why do I bother?

I stood up. "Ok, Ok, I'll get an apple, I'll get an apple. Just as I started to walk into the kitchen mom shouts....."While you up, bring me an apple."

Italian Vegetables

These sides should be in front...

Baked Spinach

Eggplant Parmesan

Italian Zucchini Sauté

Pan or Oven-Fried Asparagus

Baked Spinach

Stove top cooking
Oven at 350 degrees
Serves 4

Shopping List:
- Frozen chopped spinach
- Tomato or marinara sauce
- Ricotta & Mozzarella cheese
- Nutmeg

Ingredients

1 ½ tablespoons melted butter
½ cup onions, chopped
2 (10 oz.) packages chopped spinach
¼ cup Parmesan cheese
¾ cup Ricotta cheese
¼ teaspoon ground nutmeg
Salt and pepper to taste
⅛ teaspoon garlic powder
1 (8 oz.) can tomato sauce
½ teaspoon oregano
½ teaspoon basil
½ cup shredded mozzarella cheese (optional)

1. Cook spinach only until separated. Drain well.
2. Melt butter in large skillet over medium-high heat. Add onions and sauté until golden. Remove from heat.
3. Stir in Parmesan, Ricotta, nutmeg, salt, pepper, garlic powder, onions and spinach.
4. Spoon into 9-inch pie pan that has been sprayed with a nonstick cooking spray. Smooth top of mixture with back of a spoon.
5. *Combine tomato sauce, oregano, and basil. Spread evenly over spinach mixture. Sprinkle mozzarella cheese over top.
6. Bake, uncovered, for 25 minutes in 350 degree oven.
7. Let stand 5 minutes before serving.

***Note:** you can use a canned or homemade marinara sauce instead of tomato sauce.

Eggplant Parmesan

Stove top cooking

Oven at 350 degrees

Serves 4

Shopping List:

- 32 ounce can crushed tomatoes
- Eggplant
- Parmesan & mozzarella cheese

Ingredients

2 tablespoons olive oil + ¼ cup mixture of vegetable oil/olive oil

1 garlic clove, minced

1 large onion, finely chopped

32 ounces canned crushed tomatoes

2 teaspoons sugar or sugar substitute

½ teaspoon oregano leaves

½ teaspoon salt

1 cup dried bread crumbs

2 eggs

1 large eggplant, peeled and cut into ½ inch slices (see note)

½ cup grated Parmesan cheese

1 8-ounce mozzarella or Monterey jack cheese grated or cut into ¼ inch slices

2 tablespoon water

1. In 9-inch skillet over medium heat add 2 tablespoons oil, cook garlic and onion until tender, and then add next 5 ingredients. Reduce heat; cook, covered, 30 minutes.
2. Place bread crumbs on waxed paper. In a flat bowl, beat eggs and water. Dip eggplant slices (after salting – see note) in egg then in bread crumbs. Repeat to coat slices twice.
3. Grease 13x9 inch baking dish. In 12 inch skillet over medium heat ¼ cup mixed vegetable & olive oil, and cook a few eggplant slices at a time till golden brown. Add oil as needed.
4. Preheat oven to 350 degrees. Arrange ½ eggplant slices in baking dish. Cover with ½ tomato mixture. Sprinkle with ½ Parmesan and cheese. Repeat with the rest of eggplant slices. Bake uncovered 25 minutes.

Note: To make eggplant less bitter, after cutting, sprinkle with salt and place on a wire rack one slice upon the other. Put something heavy on the top and let the bitter juices bleed out. After 30 minutes, wash the eggplant and proceed.

Floppy Carrots?

Some things are not supposed to be limp when you want them hard.......hey, where's your mind going here.....I'm talking about vegetables. We never had fresh vegetables in the fridge. Fresh veggies have that "snap" that defines freshness; that crunch that echoes in your head as you chew. My X specialized in limp veggies. There was nothing more inviting than munching on a floppy carrot. I used to complain but she saw nothing wrong with soft celery or mushy peppers. Everything she was involved with stayed limp......I guess that's why she's my ex?

Italian Zucchini Sauté

Shopping List:
- Can of diced tomatoes
- Zucchinis

Stove top cooking
Serves 4

Ingredients

¼ cup olive oil

1 small white onion, sliced into thin wedges

1 (14.5 ounce) can diced tomatoes with juice

2 zucchinis, sliced thin

½ tablespoon Italian seasonings (oregano, basil & thyme)

1 teaspoon salt

1 teaspoon sugar

1. Heat the olive oil in a skillet over medium heat. Stir in onion and cook until tender.
2. Mix in tomatoes with juice and zucchini. Season with Italian seasoning and salt.
3. Cook and stir until zucchini is tender. Mix in sugar and adjust seasonings to taste.

Asparagus

To put it simply, asparagus makes your pee smell funny—at least it makes mine smell funny. For years, I never put two and two together.....I had dinner at Momma's, she'd make her pan-fried asparagus..... I'd get home, go to tinkle....two sniffs and I was convinced I had a bladder infection.

One night we were all at Momma's, she made her pan- fried asparagus again, my cousin Vito goes pee-pee and forgot to flush, when he finished, I walked into the bathroom and lo and behold—either he had the same bladder infection as I did or.............................could it be????? Is it possible?????? Something we ate makes your pee smell funny????

The following day, I went to the library (1960's BC—before computers) I looked up: "**....foods that make your pee smell funny....**" Yep, there it was. ASPARAGUS was the culprit. I didn't dare tell Momma for that would imply that something she cooked caused a problem and based upon the commotion that happened after Uncle Paulie told her that her Pinole nuts gave him diarrhea--------I'd just enjoy Momma's pan- fried asparagus and live with stinky pee.

Pan or Oven-Fried Asparagus

Stove top or Oven at 450 degrees
Serves 4

Ingredients

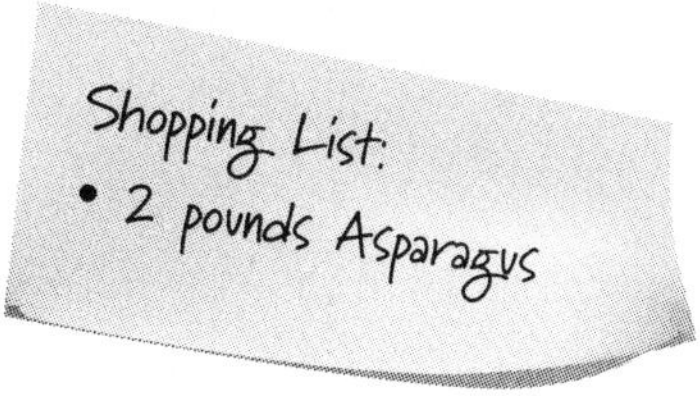

¼ cup butter or butter spray
(Depends which version you use)

2 tablespoons olive oil

1 teaspoon coarse salt

¼ teaspoon ground black pepper

3 cloves garlic, minced

2 pounds fresh asparagus spears, trimmed

Version 1

1. Melt butter in a skillet over medium-high heat. Stir in the olive oil, salt, and pepper.
2. Cook garlic in butter for a minute, but do not brown.
3. Add asparagus, and cook for 10 minutes, turning asparagus to ensure even cooking.

Version 2 (no butter or oil)

1. Spray cookie sheet with butter or olive oil spray
2. Lay asparagus in singe layer on cookie sheet & spray with oil
3. Sprinkle coarse salt over and bake at 425 degrees for about 8 – 10 minutes.

Italian pastries

My family would wait for dessert like feeding time at the zoo. A fine cannoli, that Italian delicacy with a crispy crust and a sweet cheesy filling...well, my cousin Paulie would dunk it into espresso and consider that a nutritious breakfast. That was back then when he only weighed 375 pounds.

Italian Desserts

Did you eat all your veggies?

Biscuit Tortoni

Cantucci or Biscotti

Panna Cotta

Tiramisu

Memory from Jane's childhood...

It's not exactly the same as what I remember from my childhood. But from all my experimentation, it resembles the texture and flavor of my favorite dessert served at Capri's Italian Restaurant. Sometimes, the chef at Capri's added rum flavoring to the mixture. I prefer almond. The best!

Bisque Tortoni

No cooking

Serves 4

Ingredients

2 cups vanilla ice cream.
(The higher the fat content, the better)

¼ cup Mascarpone cheese

2 tablespoons almond paste

1 teaspoon almond flavoring

½ cup crumbled & sieved macaroons or crushed almond cookies

½ cup mini-chocolate chips (optional)

1. Slightly melt the vanilla ice cream. Start to beat.
2. Add the Mascarpone & almond paste. Continue to beat until light and fluffy.
3. Fold in chocolate.
4. Place 1 tablespoon of almond crumbs in paper cups (muffin cups) or in 2 ounce paper cups. Pack in the ice cream mixture.
5. Sprinkle tops with macaroon/almond cookie crumbs.
6. Freeze until firm. Do not stir. Let stand 5 - 10 minutes before serving.

Cantucci or Biscotti

Oven at 350 degrees

Makes 2 Dozen

Ingredients

1 cup whole, raw almonds

2 cups all-purpose flour

1 ½ teaspoons baking powder

⅛ teaspoons salt

½ teaspoons cinnamon

6 tablespoons butter softened

⅔ cup of confectioners' (powdered) sugar

2 large eggs

1 tablespoons almond extract

1. Place the almonds in a preheated 325-degree F. oven and toast until they begin to take on color. Cool, and coarsely chop.
2. Mix together the flour, baking powder, cinnamon, and salt. Set aside.
3. In a large bowl, with an electric mixer, beat together the butter and powdered sugar.
4. Add the almonds, the eggs and extract.
5. Add the dry ingredients and continue mixing until well blended.
6. On a lightly floured surface, divide the dough in half, and form two loaves about 9 inches long and 2 ½ inches wide and place on a lightly greased baking sheet.
7. Bake for about 35 minutes or until they are slightly golden brown.
8. Allow to cool for 5 minutes, then using a serrated knife cut into ½ inch slices.
9. Place these slices back on the baking sheet, and cook an additional 5-10 minutes or until the cookies are golden in color and dry.
10. Store in a cool dry place.

Espresso

You weren't finished with a meal until Grandpa (yes Grandpa) served espresso. To me, this was brown mud that vaguely resembled coffee—coffee syrup. Bitter would be a euphemism for what it tasted like---to me! Grandpa would say, "You drink-a this...you get-a hair on you chest." It worked. All my cousins drank espresso and they had plenty of hair....especially my cousin RoseAnn.

Panna Cotta*

Stove top cooking
Serves 4 - 6

Shopping List:
- Unflavored gelatin
- Heavy cream or half & half

Ingredients

⅓ cup skim milk
1 (.25 ounce) envelope unflavored gelatin
**2 ½ cups heavy cream
½ cup white sugar
1 ½ teaspoons vanilla extract

1. Pour milk into a small bowl, and stir in the gelatin powder. Set aside.
2. In a saucepan, stir together the heavy cream and sugar, and set over medium heat. Bring to a full boil, watching carefully, as the cream will quickly rise to the top of the pan.
3. Pour the gelatin and milk into the cream, stirring until completely dissolved. Cook for one minute, stirring constantly. Add vanilla and stir.
4. Remove from heat, and pour into six individual ramekin dishes.
5. Cool the ramekins uncovered at room temperature. When cool, cover with plastic wrap, and refrigerate for at least 4 hours, but preferably overnight before serving.

***Note:** This is a lovely, soft pudding that goes well with most dishes. It also has no eggs for those of us who can't or don't eat eggs.

****Note:** I have made this recipe with both heavy cream & half & half. It is much creamier with heavy cream but perfectly acceptable with the half & half. I have also substituted sugar replacement for real sugar and it just isn't as sweet or good. So use the real sugar…it's only ½ cup for the entire recipe.

DESSERT STORY

My Jewish Grandma was a pip. One night, Grandma invited half of Brooklyn over for dinner—a common practice. Unfortunately, that half also invited the balance of the population of Brooklyn over to Grandma's. Now, Grandma always cooked for the preverbal Army but in this instance, she didn't expect two squadrons; she didn't have enough of anything to go around. She called all my cousins into the kitchen—6 of us and she said, "When the food comes out ...all of you say you had lots of candy in the movies and you're not hungry...." We all sat down; the cousins were at the "children's" table of course. And, as each and every delicious morsel of food was presented to my cousins and me; we had the same story. "We had too much candy at the movies...." It worked out perfectly. There was now plenty of food for the battalion of hungry adults and Grandma was not embarrassed for under preparing for the scores of surprise guests that came to dinner. The dishes were cleared—and now dessert! Grandma announces..." We have homemade cake.....for everybody but...............since the children refused to eat the chicken....they get no dessert!" Ya can't win!

The dessert of desserts!

A veritable medley of flavors. If you follow this recipe closely, very closely; the results will be outstanding. Jane and I once attempted to make Tiramisu and being both cocky and culinary neophytes we assumed we knew what we were doing. Everything was going along fine until we came to the part where you add the mascarpone. Jane didn't know what it was (an Italian cheese) and I was too "macho" to admit I didn't either. I told her, quite confidently, "Oh... that's a sweet Italian wine. So...when the recipe said, "add three cups of mascarpone (the cheese), since we didn't have real mascarpone "wine" I told her to substitute the mascarpone with three cups of Gallo Rose.

The dessert never congealed. With that amount of alcohol, it remained a slushy mixture. We took it from the fridge and tasted it. It was yummy; weird but yummy. Essentially, this was a cake you ate with a straw. Ever get drunk on a cake? We did! MASCARPONE IS A CHEESE!

Tiramisu

Tiramisu literally translates as "pick me up".

No cooking

Serves 4

Ingredients

18 ounces Mascarpone cheese at room temperature

1 ½ cups whipping cream

1 ¼ cups espresso coffee, cooled

½ cup sugar

⅓ cup brandy

24 Savoiardi cookies (Ladyfingers) or Italian sponge cake

dark chocolate, shaved

Shopping List:
- Mascarpone cheese
- Heavy cream
- Brandy
- Italian Ladyfingers
- Dark chocolate

1. Slowly beat in ½ cup of sugar into the mascarpone cheese.
2. Whip the cream until soft peaks form, and fold this into the cheese mixture.
3. Add the brandy to the cooled coffee.
4. Carefully dip in ladyfingers one at a time into the coffee mixture just until the outside of the cookie is barely damp. Arrange cookies side by side in a dish large enough to hold 12 cookies flat.
5. After the first 12 are layered, spread ½ of the cheese mixture on top.
6. Sprinkle with enough shaved chocolate to cover lightly, and repeat these layers once more topping the dish with the remaining chocolate.
7. Refrigerate several hours before serving.

Note: Be careful not to over saturate the cookies with the coffee mixture, or you will end up with a runny Tiramisu.

Some basic items needed in a Jewish Kitchen

Food Stuff:

Matzo meal, Wide Noodles

Vegetables: Celery, Carrots, Onions, Potatoes

Seasonings: Onion powder, Kosher salt, Sour salt, Black pepper

Eggs

Prunes

Honey

Vegetable Oil

White Vinegar

Utensils:

Giant Wooden Spoon, Fry pan

My how the generations have changed. When I went into the kitchen at my Bubbies' (I was allowed in THAT kitchen) I'd watch her create all these wonderful Jewish dishes—from scratch! She'd open a dozen jars with all kinds of stuff—spices, I assumed. For that matter, some of it might have been Pot . Who knew? Who asked? Nothing had labels. A pinch of this, a smidge of that. Everyday things in her kitchen had Yiddish names: A gyple (fork) A lefel (spoon) A tup (pot....the cookware) a messer (knife) a gloz (a glass) Tzuker (sugar) Teler (plate) Schmaltz (chicken fat....the Crisco of the Kosher home) Everything worked just fine in Bubbie's kitchen.

She'd say, "Tatella (little one) hand me the messer and a gyple. I grew up thinking that a fork was a gyple........everywhere. Who knew from the word "fork." Dining out was wonderful. "Excuse me waitress, there's lipstick on my gyple. My case comes up Tuesday.

MY FATHER'S JEWISH RECIPES

My Mother's Kitchen

As a kid, I was never allowed in my mother's kitchen; not because I'd eat anything edible; hence my adult propensity for plumpness, but simply because I was a (as my mother coined it) a "gagootz." That's Italian for: squash...the vegetable not the verb. A squash you might ask? You see, if you called somebody a "gagootz" you were really saying that they were "dumb like a squash."

My problem.....accidents in the kitchen. The Jewish side of the family called me a klutz. Different languages, same concept. Either way, I was a mess in the kitchen. Something always spilled, exploded. I always found the salt shaker with the loose top; the five pound bag of flour with the ripped bottom---that was a classic! We had to bring in one of those disaster relief teams to clean that one up. The whole family wheezed and coughed flour for a year. I was once pureeing tomatoes in the blender and forgot to put the top back on....the painters worked out a time payment deal with my parents.

More later..........

Jewish Soups

You'll never miss Campbell's again

Low-Fat Matzo Balls with Broth

Mushroom Barley

Pea Soup

Sweet & Sour Cabbage Soup

Italian Matzo Balls?

Wow I really loved these. Mom, made them with an Italian flair...lots of pepper. She once tried making them with oregano; my father considered this an act of international terrorism and financial sanctions were initiated. Also watch the amount of water you use; too much and you wind up with matzo-sludge; too little and you got matzo-gummies. So, follow this simple recipe carefully and you'll make "perfect" matzo balls each and every time.

Low fat* Matzo Balls in Chicken Soup

Stove top cooking
10 matzo balls
3 cups chicken broth

Ingredients for Matzo Balls

½ cup matzo meal
4 egg whites, slightly beaten
2 tablespoons vegetable canola oil
2 tablespoons water
¼ teaspoon salt

1. Combine all ingredients and put into refrigerator for 20 minutes
2. Shape into 10 balls
3. Boil in 3 cups hot chicken soup or chicken bouillon for 20 minutes
4. They may be made ahead and reheated

***Note 1:** These matzo balls are low fat because we are not using the egg yolk (which has all the fat).

Note 2: For firmer matzo balls increase the amount of matzo meal. For softer balls, increase the number of egg whites. For the softest balls use stiffly beaten egg whites.

Ingredients for Chicken Soup

1. You can either make homemade chicken broth OR
2. Use cans of chicken broth. "Doctoring" the canned soup is easy. Just add chopped carrots, celery & a bay leaf and simmer for an hour. You can either leave in the vegetables (take out the bay leaf) or if you are a purist take all the veggies out. Steve like his veggies pureed so I use the hand processor to make a smooth slightly thickened soup base for the matzo balls.
3. Add the matzo balls to the broth and serve with chopped parsley on top.

Mushroom Barley Soup

Stove top cooking

Serves 6 – 8

Shopping List:
- Dried mushrooms, button mushrooms
- Barley
- Beef bullion
- Fresh parsley

Ingredients

2 medium onions, chopped

3 cloves garlic, chopped

1 ounce dried mushrooms

16 oz mushrooms, chopped
(you can use any kind – try a variety)

1 cup whole barley (not the instant kind)

1 quart water

1 quart beef bouillon, beef broth

1 bay leaf

Salt to taste

2 teaspoons canola or olive oil

½ teaspoon ground white pepper to taste, bay leaf

Chopped parsley

1. Sauté onions and garlic in oil until limp (about 5 minutes)
2. Add 1 cup of barley
3. Add liquids, bay leaf
4. Cover and cook on low/med heat (it should be a slow boil) for 1 hour
5. While soup is cooking, soak dried mushrooms.
6. After 1 hour add mushrooms (chop reconstituted and button/variety).
7. Cook an additional 30 minutes
8. Use a hand processor to make soup fairly smooth (as smooth as you like)
9. Season with salt & pepper to taste
10. To improve flavor, refrigerate overnight. Reheat. When serving, sprinkle parsley on top.

Make the day before and reheat. Serve with pumpernickel, rye bread or pita crisps (see recipe)

Marvin's Health Advice

Poppa had a cousin named Marvin Dickman, you can only imagine how, as a kid, he was tortured for that name. Marvin was a health food nut (no pun intended). He would come to dinner at Momma's or Grandma's and watch everything being cooked in either chicken fat or lard—mostly meats. He weighed ninety pounds at best and he would sit there picking at the Pinole nuts and bread crusts lecturing everyone on the dangers of red meat, grease and oils in your diet. "You don't need that stuff in your body!" He'd proclaim. Momma and Grandma would cook away paying no mind to his oil-free tirades.

The moral? Momma died at ninety three, Grandma died at ninety two and Marvin, who suffered from chronic diverticulitis (Pinole nuts?) died at fifty six---go figure!

Pea soup

Always a surprise and always delicious. My Aunt would embellish her pea soups with anything from hotdogs to flanken....that's a Jewish type of brisket that most gourmets consider a waste product from the slaughter house. But in the hands of Aunt Sophie, the flanken in her pea soup became "the prize at the bottom of the Cracker-Jacks box." Just two bites of her flankin and you understood the concept of gastric reflux. So, stay away from the flankin and just make the soup. You'll love it.

Pea Soup

Stove top cooking

Serves 6 – 8

Shopping List:

- Dried peas
- Beef bullion

Ingredients

2 stalks celery, chopped

3 cloves garlic, chopped

2 onions, chopped

2 carrots, sliced

1 bag (10 oz) dried green peas

1 quart water

1 quart beef bouillon, beef broth

salt & pepper, to taste

1. Sauté celery, onions, garlic, & carrots until limp (about 5 minutes)
2. Add bag of peas (wash & pick through before adding to pot)
3. Add liquids
4. Cover and cook on low/med head (it should be a slow boil) for 1 ½ hours
5. Season to taste
6. Use a hand processor to puree the soup. It should be a fairly smooth consistency
7. You can add a cooked frankfurter or chopped ham (if you're not kosher) to each bowl for a more filling soup.

Make the day before and reheat. Serve with pumpernickel, rye bread or pita crisps

Now I love it!

Once again....as a kid I really didn't like this soup.... but as a kid, my idea of fine dining was Oscar Meyer Bologna and M&Ms.....no peanuts! I did have a somewhat refined palate back then.

When Grandma made this soup, the aromas permeated the neighborhood. People would follow the fragrance right back to the kitchen window. And the fragrance of the soup was only surpassed by its taste. Bubbie would cook enough to feed the entire extended family of 12 three times over. One caveat, after 12 people, in one small room, finished a bowl of Bubbies' Sweet and Sour Cabbage soup and then had seconds.... Well, there were other aromas and fragrances we all had to contend with. But, as usual, everyone blamed the dog.

Sweet & Sour Cabbage Soup

Stove top cooking

Serves 6 – 8

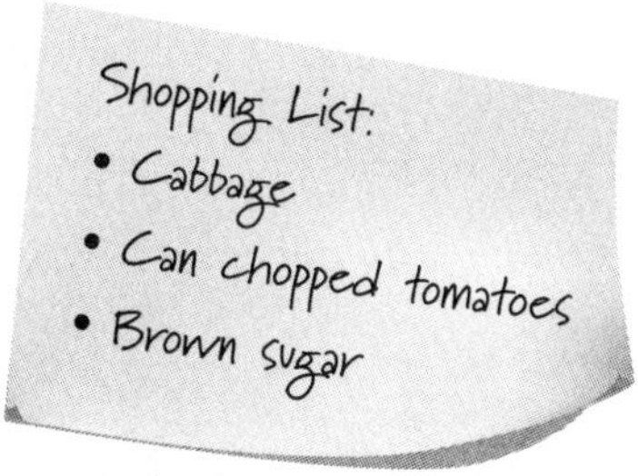

Ingredients

2 onions, chopped

2 potatoes, chopped

2 stalks celery, chopped

3 carrots, chopped

2 pounds cabbage, chopped or shredded

1 can 68 oz. chopped tomatoes plus 1 can water

2 quarts liquid (water, beef bouillon, beef broth or combination)

1 tsp salt

½ tsp white pepper

¼ cup lemon juice or apple cider vinegar to taste

2 – 3 Tablespoons brown or white sugar (you can use splenda – it comes in a brown sugar substitute). I like brown sugar best in this recipe.

1. Sauté onions, potatoes, celery, carrots until limp (about 5 minutes)
2. Add cabbage and sauté 5 more minutes
3. Add tomatoes, liquid and cook about 1 hour
4. After cooked, season with salt, pepper, lemon or vinegar, and sugar to taste
5. If you like a more processed soup, you can run it through the food processor
6. If you like sour cream (or yogurt), you can add a dollop to each bowl before serving.

Better if you make the day before and reheat.

Is it chicken or beef?

My Bubbie would buy inexpensive cuts of meat from our butcher. He'd hold them aside for her to pick up just prior to them being sent off to the dog-food factory. She would cut it up, beat it up, pull off the delicious strands of fats, grizzle and sinew, then marinate the meats in her own special ingredients and cook them to perfection. Nobody ever asked "what part of the cow was this from?" The brown sauce that covered the meat usually hid its cosmetic imperfections and it always tasted fine. We kept quiet...we were young but not stupid and besides....Bubbies' wooden spoon had multiple uses.

Jewish Entrees

Let the games begin

Brisket

Honey-Apple Glazed Turkey Breast

Sole Rollups

Salmon Croquettes

Brisket

Stove top or Oven cooking – 325 degrees
Serves 6 - 8

Version 1 Ingredients

1 - 5 pound brisket. I use the flat cut which is leaner and has less grizzle. You can also use shoulder roast of beef, chuck roast or end of steak

3 Tablespoons flour

2 garlic cloves, peeled & minced

2 tablespoons vegetable oil

2 cups water

3 onions, peeled & diced

6 to 8 carrots, peeled & sliced on the diagonal

2 stalks celery, chopped

1 package onion soup mix

Version 1 – The easy way

1. Dredge meat in flour then brown in the oil
2. Add the garlic & onions around the meat & sauté until limp
3. Add the onion soup mix & water. Simmer on top of the stove for 1 hour
4. Add the carrots & celery after 1 hour
5. Continue cooking on the stove about 2 hours more or until tender

Version 2 Ingredients

1 - 5 pound brisket. I use the flat cut which is leaner and has less grizzle. You can also use shoulder roast of beef, chuck roast or end of steak

Salt & pepper

2 cloves of garlic, peeled & cut in half

3 tablespoons flour

3 onions, peeled & diced

1 – 14.5 ounce can of tomatoes (I prefer chopped)

2 stalks celery, chopped

6 to 8 carrots, peeled & sliced on the diagonal

½ can water

½ cup red wine

¼ cup chopped parsley, 1 teaspoon thyme,

3 small bay leaves & 1 sprig rosemary

Version 2 – Not as easy

1. Sprinkle salt & pepper over the brisket & rub with garlic. Dredge meat in flour.
2. Sear the brisket in the oil and place fat side up in a large casserole. Sprinkle onions on top & sides of the meat.
3. Cover with tomatoes, red wine, water, bay leaf, thyme & rosemary
4. Cover & bake in a preheated 325 degree oven for about 3 hours. Baste with juices
5. Add parsley, celery, carrots & bake, uncovered, for about 30 minutes more until carrots are cooked.

In both cases, it is best to cook a day or two ahead. This way, you can skim the fat from the surface before reheating. Cut the brisket on a cutting board. Look for the grain and cut across it. Serve with farfel (boiled egg barley noodles), noodle kugel or potato pancakes.

Honey Apple Glazed Turkey Breast

Oven 325 degrees

Serves 6 – 8

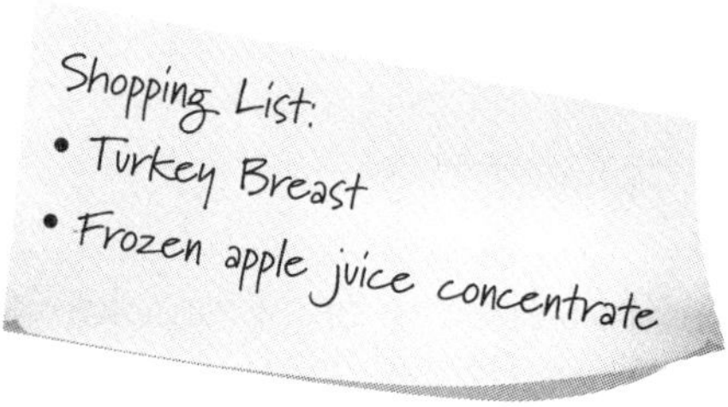

Ingredients

⅓ cup honey

1 tablespoon dry mustard

1 (6-½ to 7 pound) turkey breast,
skin and all visible fat removed

1 x 6 ounce can frozen apple juice concentrate, thawed and undiluted

1. Combine honey, mustard and apple juice in a bowl, stirring well. Set aside.
2. Place turkey breast in roasting pan, insert meat thermometer into meaty portion so that it does not touch the bone. Baste with honey mixture.
3. Cover and bake at 325 degrees Fahrenheit for 1 hour. Uncover and bake an additional hour or until meat thermometer registers 170 degrees, basting frequently with the honey sauce mixture that accumulates in pan.

   (Total baking time is approximately 2 hours, ovens may vary).
4. Let cool at least 15-20 minutes before slicing.

Sole Rollups

This is an easy fish recipe. You may use sole, tilapia or another lightweight white fish filet for this fabulous dairy dish.

Oven cooking at 350 degrees

Shopping List:
- *2 pounds of Fillet of sole*

Ingredients

2 lbs. sole fillets (you can use any sweet white fish like flounder or basa)

½ cup cracker crumbs

¼ cup melted butter or margarine

½ cup grated yellow cheese

1 tbsp. Worcestershire sauce

1 tbsp. lemon juice

1 tsp. Dijon mustard

Salt, pepper, paprika, to taste

Fresh herbs, if desired

1. Rinse fish, pat dry with paper towels and set aside.
2. Mix together the remaining ingredients, including salt, pepper and paprika*.
3. Place a bit more than 1 tablespoon of the cracker mixture on each fish fillet. Leave a border around the fish fillet so that filling will not spill out.
4. Roll up each fish fillet and secure with a toothpick or two.
5. You may sprinkle a bit of salt, pepper and herbs over the top of the fish fillets, if desired.
6. Place sole rollups in a lightly greased baking dish and sprinkle leftover mixture over the top.
7. Preheat oven to 350 degrees F.
8. Bake for 30 minutes and serve. Roll-ups make a delicious main course or they can also be served as an appetizer.

***Note:** You may increase quantities of filling ingredients to have extra topping.

Salmon Croquettes

Thursday was Salmon croquette day. I dreaded Thursdays. "Salmon! Salmon again? Mom didn't you read that they found out that Salmon is poisonous to small kids?" After a few choice words (mostly in Italian) I realized that it would be beneficial for me to immediately run out of the kitchen before she made Steve croquettes.

As a kid, I hated Salmon Croquettes. As an adult, I can't believe what a schmuck I was....These are delicious and easy to make.

Salmon Croquettes with dill

Oven cooking – 400 degrees
8 croquettes – serves 4

Shopping List:
- Salmon
- Scallions
- Fresh parsley & dill

Ingredients

2 slices white bread
1 ½ pounds boneless, skinless salmon fillet*
4 scallions, finely chopped
2 tablespoons chopped fresh dill
2 tablespoons finely chopped fresh parsley
1 clove garlic, minced
½ teaspoon freshly grated lemon rind
½ cup egg substitute or 1 egg & 2 egg whites
Salt & freshly ground pepper

1. Lightly spray a nonstick baking sheet with spray oil. Place the baking sheet in the oven and preheat to 400 degrees.
2. Soak bread in warm water for 3 minutes. Squeeze the bread in your fingers to wring out the excess liquid. Place the bread in a mixing bowl.
3. Finely chop the salmon. In the old days you would chop by hand or use a handcrank meat grinder. Today we use a food processor. First, cut it into 1-inch pieces before chopping. Run the processor in short burst. Don't over process or you'll wind up with a spongy puree.
4. Transfer the salmon to the mixing bowl. Stir in the scallions, dill, parsley, garlic, lemon peel, egg, & salt & pepper to taste.
5. Wet your hands and form the salmon mixture into 8 3-inch balls, gently flatten each with the palm of your hand. Lightly spray the tops of the croquettes with oil
6. Bake the salmon croquettes until lightly browned and firm (10 to 15 minutes) turning the croquettes after 5 minutes
7. Serve at once.

***Note:** Don't forget to have the butcher skin the salmon.

VEGGIES???

Who knew from Veggies? Growing up in two kitchens I soon realized that Italians worked with three vegetables: Tomatoes, Onions and Mushrooms; occasionally Grandma Angelina would introduce hot peppers which introduced us to Tums. Grandma Ida worked with dozens of vegetables.....all potatoes. Potatoes were THEE vegetable. Boiled, Baked, Roasted --I liked the crispies---I always liked the crispies, deep fried in the roasting pan......when I was 42, they took out my gall bladder. I'll have the BAKED potato please.

Jewish Vegetables

Even baby cousin Moisha's gonna love these... and he hates everything!

Creamed Spinach

Grilled Veggies

Vegetable Cutlets

Tzimmes

Creamed Spinach

Stove top

Serves 6

> Shopping List:
> - Frozen or fresh spinach
> - Mushroom soup
> - Chinese noodles

Ingredients

2 pounds fresh spinach or 2 packages frozen chopped spinach

2 - 10 ounce cans of cream of mushroom soup

½ teaspoon each of onion & garlic powder

½ can of water or chicken bullion

Chinese noodles (optional)

1. Steam fresh spinach until limp (about 3 minutes) or steam the frozen spinach until cooked (about 8 minutes).
2. Drain spinach until almost dry
3. Combine soup, onion, garlic & liquid together
4. Mix in the spinach. Cook until completely heated.
5. Sprinkle Chinese noodles on top. Serve immediately

Grilled Veggies

Shopping List:

- Sweet onions
- White & sweet potato
- Portobello mushrooms
- Zucchini
- Eggplant
- Red & green peppers
- Asparagus

Oven or Barbeque cooking

Serves 6

Ingredients

1 onion (sweet), sliced

1 white & 1 sweet potato, peeled & sliced (you may want to pre-boil the potatoes for about 10 minutes before oven baking)

2 Portobello mushrooms, sliced

2 medium green zucchini, peeled & cut in strips

1 small eggplant (Italian is best) & peeled & sliced

1 red & 1 green pepper seeded & sliced

Bunch of thin asparagus, ends cut off

(Use any other veggie or combination that you like…slice or cut in thin strips)

¼ - ½ cup olive oil or olive oil & safflower oil mixed in equal parts

½ teaspoon each of garlic powder, onion powder, paprika, basil, oregano, thyme, white pepper

2 teaspoons salt

Balsamic Vinegar

1. Prepare vegetables and place into large baggies.
2. Mix oil & herbs together & pour over vegetables. Mix well in bag.
3. Place seasoned vegetables on cookie sheets. Keep them in single layer. You may need two or three trays. If barbequing, place in single layer in a device that you can turn.
4. Preheat oven to 400 - 450 degrees. Place trays in oven and cook about 10 -12 minutes. You want the vegetables to be browned.
5. When browned, take out and place on serving dish. You can serve it hot, warm or cold. You can also, if you want make a vinaigrette (or use a store-bought one) and pour over cooked vegetables.

Note 1: The oven may smoke and steam. **Be careful opening door.** The water from the vegetables quickly turns to steam and you need to open door before bending to check on the vegetables.

Note 2: I try to keep like veggies together on the same cookie sheet because some veggies cook faster than others. Potatoes may need to be pre-boiled for a few minutes before putting in oven.

Dining vs eating

Unless it was a holiday.....we ATE. We were fed; and feeding time was never gracious, formal or fussy. Food theft was prevalent in my Mom's kitchen. Twenty percent of her chicken cutlets (with the crispy crust) never made it to the table. They were either snatched up during delivery to the table. Or, and this was SO clever; a chicken cutlet would "fall" on the floor, the offender would then pretend to throw it away and in reality, tuck it aside for later. Sure, Mom would scream about how "clumsy" we were.... Sometimes the punishment is worth the crime ☺

Momma's Vegetable Cutlets

Stove top
Oven cooking 400 degrees
Makes 12 – 15 Cutlets
Serves 12 – 15 for appetizers or 4 – 6 as a main entree.

Ingredients

6 medium potatoes, peeled and cut into 2-inch cubes (about 2 pounds)
Butter spray
1 tablespoon vegetable oil
2 medium onions, chopped
6 mushrooms, chopped
1 (14 ½-ounce) can diced carrots, drained (See note 1)
1 (14 ½-ounce) can cut green beans, drained
1 (14 ½-ounce) can peas, drained
2 eggs or egg substitute
2 cups matzo meal (approximately)
Salt and freshly ground pepper

1. Preheat oven to 400 degrees
2. Cook potatoes in boiling salted water for 20 minutes, or until tender. Mash.
3. Meanwhile, in a skillet, heat butter and sauté onions and mushrooms until tender.
4. Pour mushroom mixture into a bowl with mashed potatoes. Stir in carrots, green beans, peas and 2 eggs. Blend thoroughly.
5. Add enough matzo meal so that mixture can be shaped into large patties. Season to taste with salt and pepper.
6. Shape into 12 to 15 patties. Spray patties with butter spray. Place on a well-sprayed cookie sheet.
7. Bake for 45 minutes at 400 degrees, or until lightly golden browned.
8. Serve hot with your favorite mushroom gravy or serve with low fat sour cream or Greek yogurt. Delicious!

NOTE 1: Canned diced carrots seem to be no longer available. Use sliced carrots and dice them.

Tzimmes

Oven 350 degrees

Serves 10 – 12 side servings

Ingredients

3 pounds carrots, peeled & sliced diagonally into 1-inch pieces

2 pounds yams, peeled & sliced into 2 inch circles

16 large pitted prunes cut into thirds

½ to ⅔ cup honey

1 tablespoon ground cinnamon

Freshly grated nutmeg to taste

1. Preheat oven to 350 degrees. Coat a large covered casserole with vegetable cooking spray.
2. Layer the carrots, yams & prunes alternately in the prepared pan, drizzling with honey to taste and sprinkling with the spices.
3. Add water to cover the ingredients (about 1 cup). Cover & bake 30 minutes.
4. Uncover & bake 30 additional minutes, or until the carrots & yams are soft & the liquid is reduced to a thick & slightly sticky consistency.

Jewish Starches

These carbs are allowed

Challah Bread Pudding

Kasha Varnishkas

Noodle Pudding

Sweet Potato Kugel

Challah Bread Pudding

Oven at 325 degrees
12 servings

Shopping List:
- Dried tart cherries
- Golden raisins
- Fat-free condensed milk
- Nutmeg
- Challah

Ingredients

2 ½ cups 2% low-fat milk
½ cup dried tart cherries
½ cup golden raisins
½ cup fat-free sweetened condensed milk
2 teaspoons vanilla extract
1 teaspoon ground cinnamon
½ teaspoon freshly grated nutmeg
¼ teaspoon salt
3 large eggs
8 cups (1-inch) cubes challah or other egg bread (about ½ large loaf)
Cooking spray
2 tablespoons sugar

1. Preheat oven to 325°.
2. Combine the first 9 ingredients in a large bowl.
3. Add challah cubes, tossing to coat. Let challah mixture stand 30 minutes, stirring occasionally.
4. Coat an 11 x 7-inch baking dish with cooking spray.
5. Spoon the challah mixture into dish, and sprinkle with sugar.
6. Bake at 325° for 55 minutes or until pudding is set. Let pudding stand 15 minutes before serving.

Note: This is a wonderful breakfast treat. Assemble the night before , refrigerate and cook in the morning. Yummy!

Kasha Varnishkas
(Bow tie pasta & Mushrooms)

Stove top cooking
Serves 4 - 6

Shopping List:
- Kasha
- Bow tie noodles
- Button mushrooms
- Beef or chicken broth

Ingredients

1 cup Kasha (buckwheat groats)
2 cups dry small bow tie noodles
Salt, to taste
1 tablespoon extra-virgin olive oil or vegetable oil
1 medium onion, peeled & finely chopped
1 ½ cups thinly sliced button mushrooms, shitakes or fresh porcini
1 egg white
2 cups boiling beef or chicken broth or water
Freshly ground black pepper

1. Wash the kasha under cold water. Drain & blot dry.
2. Cook bow ties in boiling salted water until al dente (6 – 8 minutes). Drain, refresh under cold water & drain again.
3. Heat the oil in a large, heavy saucepan. Add onions & mushrooms & cook over medium heat until onions are golden brown & mushrooms have lost most of their liquid (5 – 7 minutes).
4. Put cooked onions & mushrooms in a bowl to let cool
5. Add the kasha & egg white to the pan and stir well. Cook over high heat, stirring for 1 – 2 minutes until the kasha grains are dry.
6. Stir in the onion, mushroom, broth, salt & pepper.
7. In another saucepan, boil water & add bow ties. Cook until al dente. Drain.
8. Simmer the kasha, covered until tender & all the liquid is absorbed (about 15 minutes)
9. Add the bow ties the last 3 minutes. Season to taste.

Noodle Pudding

Is this dessert? Is this a side dish....Side dish? Never! Calling a noodle pudding (AKA koogle) a side dish is like saying you may get moist from a tidal wave. To paraphrase Sarah Lee: "Nobody doesn't like noodle pudding" Remember it's not just a Jewish dish. The Italian side of my family loved it too "cept they never called it "koogle"; they always tried to find an Italian name for it.... "Crispy sweet fettuccini" "Noodles-Napoli" They all ate it. They all loved it. You will too.

Ruth's Simple Noodle Kugel (Pudding)

Oven at 350 degrees

Serves 8

Ingredients

8 oz. extra wide noodles

8 oz. container low fat sour cream

8 oz. low fat cottage cheese

¾ cup sugar or sugar equivalent

1 - 2 teaspoons vanilla (depends how much you like vanilla)

1 cup raisins soaked in warm water (or a liquor)

4 eggs or egg substitute equivalent

1 cup low fat milk

1 teaspoon butter flavor (optional)

½ teaspoon cinnamon

½ cup Cornflakes (crushed)

1. Grease baking dish and soak raisins in warm water
2. Cook noodles until al dente
3. Add sour cream, cottage cheese, sugar/Splenda, vanilla, butter flavor & drained raisins to cooked noodles
4. Beat eggs add milk and pour eggs and milk into noodle mixture
5. Spread into baking dish
6. Sprinkle with cinnamon & cornflakes
7. Bake for 30 - 45 minutes until browned

Note: You can add drained pineapple, mandarin oranges, apples, pears or any combination to this basic mixture. Be creative. I've even added chocolate bits and nuts. The combinations all depend upon if this dish is to be served with the main course or for dessert.

Note 2: Leftovers are best if heated before serving

Sweet Potato Kugel

Oven at 375 degrees
Serves 12

Ingredients

6 small sweet potatoes, peeled and grated
3 apples, peeled and grated
1 cup raisins
1 cup matzo meal
2 tsp cinnamon
1 cup fruit juice or water

1. Preheat oven to 375 degrees.
2. Mix ingredients together.
3. Press into large baking dish sprayed with cooking spray.
4. Bake 45 minutes at 375 degrees until crisp on top.

Jewish Desserts

Did you call your Mother today?
OK, you can have dessert.

The Case of the Deadly Bunt Cake

People who go through a divorce are always asked. "What happened?" "When did you notice things falling apart with you two?" Few of us know the day; the straw that broke the camel's back.... I know the day and time exactly.

After being banned from kitchens most of my adolescent life for the crime of Excessive Messiness, And, after marrying a lady whose sole purpose in life was to clean and be tidy—you can see my predicament. Since I was used to being banished from Kitchens, I took no offense when my new bride followed in my mother's footsteps. My reputation preceded me.

I was watching TV one Sunday afternoon when I heard this strange grunting sound coming from my no-man's land.... AKA the kitchen. "Honey" I asked. "Are you ok?" My wife screamed back. "I can't get this bunt cake out of the pan. I have to serve it at a meeting in 1/2 hour....grunt, grunt, crap, grunt." I said, "Do you need some help in there?" My wife, still screaming; "This is a double chocolate, fudge filled bunt cake....we have a white kitchen....are you out of your mind? Grunt, shit, grunt" I peeked into the kitchen and watcher her struggle, trying desperately to loosen the cake from the pan with spatulas, knives, wooden spoons. "Are you sure I can't help?" I said sheepishly. She looked up. "Ok" she said, "come in here. BUT...if you get one crumb on the counters, the floor...anyplace...I'll kill you."

I surveyed the bunt cake, analyzing each chocolate morsel's position with respect to the pan. "Where's the serving plate that the cake will be served on," I asked. "Here, it's my grandmother's. It's an antique, be careful." She said. I moved over a small step stool so I could be about a foot or two above the counter. I turned over the double chocolate, fudge filled cake directly above the serving plate so as to catch all the crumbs. I figured Newton's second law of motion---momentum, should come into play. I assumed that if I shook and jerked the cake just right...., gravity would do the rest. It worked perfectly. I shook and jerked and the double chocolate and low and behold the fudge filled bunt cake came right out!

One small problem. I was too high. The 2 1/2 pound cake was about two feet from the plate when it left the pan. And, building up speed (thanks to gravity) it smashed down onto Grandma's antique serving plate shattering it into thousands of small shards of porcelain. Oh but there's more.... the double chocolate, fudge filled bunt cake then struck the counter with the impact of a meteor splitting open the cake and allowing the fudge to find its way into every corner and crevice of the kitchen; including, but not limited to, my wife's hair. She stood there watching too hysterical to scream...at first. I don't remember much after that. Things starting moving in slow motion. The dog stepped in fudge. She stepped in fudge. I tried to glue the cake back together using the fudge using my hand as a spatula.

Soon after, we were divorced. To this day, even if I see fudge in a store, I still twitch.

Comfort Food

Forget the looks, savor the taste. There's an expression in Yiddish: Kvell....to enjoy immensely...inner pride.... With this compote, the smell will make you kvell. One taste and you'll wonder why you bothered with the main course. Hide some for yourself in the back of the fridge. This is what defines comfort food.

Compote

Stove top cooking
10-12 servings

Shopping List:
- Dried mixed fruit
- Brandy, cognac or amaretto

Ingredients

2 packages dried mixed fruit (11 oz. size)
¼ lb dried apples
½ cup light raisins
½ cup sugar or Sweetener equivalent
2 sticks cinnamon (about 3" each)
1 tablespoon brandy, cognac or amaretto (optional)

1. Place dried fruit with cinnamon stick in a 5- qt Dutch oven or saucepan. Add 6 cups hot water to cover fruit and refrigerate covered several hours or overnight.
2. Next day, bring to boil; simmer covered until soft but not mushy (about ½ hr). Add sugar the last 5 minutes and optional liquor.
3. Remove cinnamon sticks. Refrigerate covered until well chilled or overnight.

Note: This is a dish my grandmother always made for Hanukah. I don't really know why. It's great all year and wonderful at breakfast to get things going, if you know what I mean.

Easy Carrot Cake

Easy Carrot Cake is definitely worth the effort. The combination of carrots, cinnamon, pineapple, nuts and raisins makes a fragrant, moist cake that you can eat as a dessert or snack.

Oven

Preheat oven to 350 degrees F

Ingredients

3 eggs
1 ⅓ cups sugar
1 cup oil
1 tsp. vanilla extract
½ cup crushed, drained pineapple
2 cups grated carrots
½ cup chopped nuts
½ cup raisins
½ cup flaked coconut, optional
1 tsp. baking soda
1 ½ tsp. baking powder
1 ½ tsp. cinnamon
Pinch of salt
2 cups flour

Shopping List:
- *Small can crushed pineapple*
- *Flaked coconut*

1. Grease a tube pan or two small loaf pans.
2. Beat eggs and sugar until light and fluffy. Add oil and vanilla and beat until well mixed.
3. Stir in rest of ingredients ending with the flour. Pour batter into prepared tube or loaf pans.
4. Bake for 60-70 minutes until centre of cake is firm and a toothpick comes out clean. If using smaller loaf pans, check for doneness after 45-50 minutes.

You may frost the carrot cake with cream cheese icing but frankly, it is not necessary - the cake is moist and delicious on its own.

Peach or Plum Kuchen

Oven 400 & 350 degrees

8 servings

Ingredients

5 – 6 ripe peaches or Italian plums
(I like to use both)

2 cups all-purpose flour

8 Tablespoons butter/margarine (1 stick)

½ teaspoon salt

½ - 1 cup sugar

1 cup heavy cream, half & half or yogurt

2 eggs

Cinnamon (optional)

Shopping List:

- 5 – 6 Peaches or plums (or a mixed of both)
- 1 cup heavy cream or half & half

1. Preheat oven to 400 degrees.
2. Mix together the flour, ¼ cup of sugar & salt. Set aside.
3. Cut the butter/margarine into the flour mixture using your fingertips. It should feel like coarse meal.
4. Press this mixture into the bottom & sides of a deep 9 or 10 inch pie plate
5. Put the fruit over the crust & sprinkle with ¼ - ¾ cup of sugar. This depends upon how sweet you like it. I usually use about ½ cup.
6. Bake for 15 minutes until lightly brown.
7. While baking, blend together the eggs and cream/half& half or yogurt.
8. After 15 minutes, remove the kuchen & pour the egg mixture over the fruit. Sprinkle cinnamon, if desired. Reduce heat to 350 degree.
9. Return kuchen to the oven for an additional 30 minutes. The egg mixture should be set and browned.
10. Serve warm or at room temperature.

Honey Cake

The staple dessert on the Jewish menu. Jane adds nuts and raisins....I hate nuts and raisins. Nuts give me a headache and I consider raisins geriatric grapes. But that's me! You on the other hand will love this easy to prepare treat and your guests will swear you bought this delight at some sophisticated pastry shop. Don't modify the recipe. It'll come out perfectly. I do give you dispensation for leaving out the nuts and raisins.

I guess my dislike of raisins goes back to when I was a kid and couldn't eat chocolate; I got headaches from that too. So my mother decided that a small box of raisins (raisins have a shelf life of 30 years) is candy. Yep raisins to the left of me, raisins to the right....

All my friends enjoyed Milky Ways, Snickers, Clark Bars....Me? I was stuck with raisins that crunched like they came over on the Mayflower.

Honey Cake

Oven 325 degrees
12 servings

Shopping List:
- Walnuts
- Raisins
- Instant coffee
- Honey

Ingredients

Cooking spray
1 tablespoon dry breadcrumbs
¼ cup hot water
2 teaspoons instant espresso granules or
4 teaspoons instant coffee granules
½ cup sugar or sweetener equivalent
2 large eggs
½ cup honey
3 tablespoons stick margarine, melted
1 ¾ cups all-purpose flour
1 teaspoon baking powder
1 teaspoon ground cinnamon
¼ teaspoon salt
½ cup walnuts, chopped
½ cup golden raisins

1. Preheat oven to 325°.
2. Coat an 8 x 4-inch loaf pan with cooking spray, and dust with breadcrumbs; set pan aside.
3. Combine water and coffee granules, and set aside.
4. Combine sugar and eggs in a medium bowl; stir well with a whisk. Add honey and margarine; stir well.
5. In another bowl, combine flour, baking powder, cinnamon, and salt.
6. Add half of flour mixture to sugar mixture; stir well.
7. Add coffee mixture; stir well.
8. Add remaining flour mixture, and stir just until flour mixture is moist.
9. Stir in walnuts and raisins.
10. Spoon cake batter into prepared loaf pan, and bake at 325° for 1 hour and 20 minutes or until a wooden pick inserted in center of cake comes out clean.

Cool cake in pan 10 minutes on a wire rack, and remove from pan. Cool cake completely on wire rack.

Equivalent Measurements & Herb Guide

Volume (Liquid)

Standard 1 cup = 8 oz.

Imp. Oz	US Cups	Metric g
1	⅛	28
2	¼	56
3	⅜	84
4	½	112
5	⅝	140
6	¾	168
7	⅞	196
8	1	224
9	1 ⅛	252
10	1 ¼	280
11	1 ⅜	308
12	1 ½	336
13	1 ⅝	364
14	1 ¾	392
15	1 ⅞	420
16	2	448
17	2 ⅛	476
18	2 ¼	504

American Standard (Cups & Quarts)	American Standard (Ounces)	Metric (Milliliters & Liters)
2 teaspoons	1 fluid ounce	30 ml
¼ cup	2 fluid ounces	60 ml
½ cup	4 fluid ounces	125 ml
1 cup	8 fluid ounces	250 ml
1 ½ cups	12 fluid ounces	375 ml
2 cups or 1 pint	16 fluid ounces	500 ml
4 cups or 1 quart	32 fluid ounces	1000 ml or 1 liter
1 gallon	128 fluid ounces	4 liters

Small can

1 lb. 450 g 2 cups

Large Can

2 lb. 3 oz. 1 kg. 250 g 4 cups

Liquids

Imp. Fl. Oz.	UK pints	US pints	US quarts	US cups	Metric g
2	-	-	-	¼	56
4	-	¼	-	½	120
5	¼	-	-	-	140
8	-	½	-	1	225
10	½	-	-	1 ¼	280
12	-	¾	-	1 ½	340
16	-	1	-	2	455
20	1	1 ¼	-	2 ½	570
32	-	2	1	4	910

Dry Measure Equivalents

3 teaspoons	1 tablespoon	½ ounce	14.3 grams
2 tablespoons	⅛ cup	1 ounce	28.3 grams
4 tablespoons	¼ cup	2 ounces	56.7 grams
5 ⅓ tablespoons	⅓ cup	2.6 ounces	75.6 grams
8 tablespoons	½ cup	4 ounces	113.4 grams
12 tablespoons	¾ cup	6 ounces	.375 pound
32 tablespoons	2 cups	16 ounces	1 pound

Herb Guide

Herb	Flavor	Great with	Notes
Basil	Fragrant & spicy- almost peppery	Tomatoes, vegetables, poultry, grilled pizza & salads.	Best used as whole leaves or torn. Smaller leaves at top of bunch are the sweetest.
Chives	Subtle onion sometimes spicy with grasslike leaves	Egg dishes, soups, sauces, baked potatoes, & fish.	Snip with scissors for best results.
Cilantro	A lively flavor; soapy, some say: looks similar to flat-leaf parsley	Asian, Mexican & Indian dishes; mix in salsas & chutneys.	Leaves become bitter after plant flowers. Dried seeds are the spice coriander.

Herb	Flavor	Great with	Notes
Dill	Fresh & grassy.	Tuna salad, omelets, vegetables, seafood dishes, yogurt dressing for cucumbers, & herb vinegars	Use dill fresh or add to hot food just before serving
Mint	Cool; brightens up both savory & sweet dishes	Beverages, jellies, sauces, marinades for meat & vegetables.	The most popular variety is spearmint. To dry, hang in a dark place with low humidity
Oregano	Earthy; balances acidic tomatoes – hence common on pizza	Lamb, beef, eggs, bean, eggplant, tomatoes	Related to marjoram (but more elegant) so they aren't classified separately
Parsley	Peppery & fresh; curly parsley is milder than flat-leaf Italian	Salads, vegetables (especially potatoes); soup & pasta	Either variety is a breath freshener.
Rosemary	Pungent aroma & pine flavor	Mediterranean dishes, lamb, poultry, fish, breads.	When grilling, sturdier stems make good skewers.
Sage	Very aromatic & woody	Holiday stuffing for turkey or chicken, seasons rich meats like pork, goose, & duck	Deep-fried sage is a lovely garnish
Tarragon	Hints of licorice	Poultry, fish, shellfish, vegetables, vinegar & eggs	Two types; French is preferred over the more bitter Russian
Thyme	Minty & citrusy	Mediterranean dishes, stews, eggs, seafood, poultry & tomatoes	Strip leaves from stems by pulling through fork tines.

Adapted from Good Housekeeping, August, 2006 page 152

Looking back, I smile

My Kitchen-related crimes are too numerous to mention. Things happened to me that, to this day, people think I make up. As a child, I was so prone to kitchen disasters that, statistically, I was un-insurable. If a grand prize need be awarded for a kitchen act so horrific it would be awarded to and still (50 years later) is referred to as the..."**remember what happened to Steve just before Passover**" incident.

Mom was having Dad's entire family over for Passover Dinner. Mom cooked for almost three years in preparation for this feast. The Fridge was over-stuffed with goodies and Mom made Jello..... red Jello. Ask any kid...green or yellow Jello's NOT Jello. Plus, I convinced her to buy Redi-Whip instant whipped cream. Wow!

It was Sunday, I got up early, went into the TV room and turned on cartoons; my parents were sleeping. I went to make some cereal but when I opened the Fridge to get milk....there it was, the Jello! Jello for breakfast? Why not? My cereal bowl became my Jello bowl. But wait....there's the Redi-whip. I scooped out some Jello, took off the Redi-whip top and placed a dollop, ok, maybe a mound of Redi-whip on the Jello. I took the redi-whip and wedged the can back into the fridge. I was sitting at the table just finishing my scrumptious Jello breakfast when I heard this "squishing-gurgling" sound come from the Kitchen. I looked around for a bit. Then I opened the Fridge and you guessed it. A bottle of Manishevitz wine was leaning against the nozzle and Redi-Whip had filled the first two shelves of the Fridge. I grabbed towels, some cleaning stuff and worked away. My Dad heard the commotion. He saw my face, knew what happened and helped clean up the mess. He said he'd take care of me after Passover.

I started thinking about the "death of the first born son" scenario. To this day, the family wonders how the brisket had that...fresh pine scent.

About Steve...

A native of Brooklyn, Steve grew up in the multi-ethnic neighborhood of Sheepshead Bay. This was the perfect training ground for a dialectician. As the class clown and as a very authentic sounding Chinese restaurant delivery boy, Steve learned at an early age how to use his gift for imitating accents to his advantage.

Using humor, dialect and sound effects in teaching, Steve was a real life version of Gabe Kaplan's "Welcome Back Kotter." Eventually, Steve became Assistant to the Superintendant of Schools on Long Island, New York. He also discovered he had an incredible aptitude for business and started building telecommunications systems.

He left this tremendous academic and business success behind and turned his attention to his latent love of making people laugh. As Steve puts it,"I was sick and tired of the regular pay-checks, the prestige and the educational glamour of an Administrator's life so I decided to get on the road and make 30 dollars a show."

"My Mother's Italian, My Father's Jewish & I'm in Therapy" opened at The Little Schubert Theatre on 42nd Street, November 3, 2006. The show ran in New York for almost two years. It's now one of the longest running one-man-shows in Broadway history.

Since Broadway, Steve went back on the road. He's spent his spare time writing two more shows; "My Mother's Italian, My Father's Jewish & I'm **Still** in Therapy", in 2008 and "My Mother's Italian, My Father's Jewish & I'm Home for the Holidays" in 2010.

In 2009, an International Production Company started touring the first show, "My Mother's Italian, My Father's Jewish & I'm in Therapy" in South Africa. Canada, Great Britain, New Zealand and Australia are being scheduled as this revised cookbook is being printed.

Also in 2009, a national touring company began producing "My Mother's Italian, My Father's Jewish & I'm in Therapy." The touring company uses other actors/comedians and has played in Phoenix, AZ, Philadelphia, PA Columbus, OH, San Diego, CA & Toronto, Canada. Many more venues are being planned for the 2013 – 2014 Season.

Steve is now working on an audio book about his hilarious life adventures and he just completed the CD of "...Home for the Holidays." Steve continues to find new ways to entertain the wonderful audiences and fans who support live theatre and attend all his shows. This adventure in comedy is Steve's dream come true.

About Jane...

Jane was born in Manhattan and lived her first 50 years on Long Island. Her mission in life: "To learn as much as I can and have fun doing it."

So far, she's been an Educator (High School English)...Audio Visual & Multimedia producer, owner & creative Director (Parallax Studio, Ltd.)...marketing direct (MBA)... Corporate Communications Director, President (The Karis Company, Inc.)... Adjunct professor of marketing & media (FAU)... interior re-designer (I.R.I.S.)... Jewelry designer... suicide prevention volunteer... associate webmaster ... community emergency response team member & author (Forgotten Women - Ancient Times, My Mother's Italian, My Father's Jewish & I'm in Therapy Cookbook (first & second edition).

As a lifelong creative chef, Jane has spent decades adapting recipes, and attempting to encourage Steve, a less than adventurous foodie, to experiment with new food combinations. She has gotten him to try and almost tolerate Thai and even some Ethiopian cuisines, but he always resorts back to Mama's favorite dishes. I've modified all the delicious recipes to keep him healthy.

In her spare time, Jane is pursuing her artistic ambitions by taking a variety of art classes. Tomorrow, she begins paint pouring (remember Jackson Pollack?). Steve had better watch where he walks. You never know where that paint will land.

In my family, chaos was the way of life; loving chaos in bits and pieces. Total chaos broke out at family dinners. Grandma Ida (the Jewish matriarch and national spokeswoman for chicken fat and Crisco) had her opinions of Grandma Angelina's cooking (the criminal abuser of grated cheese) and visa versa. My Dad had a rule that no one could argue during dinner... thus, dinner usually ended abruptly allowing ample time for family debates.

I was convinced that both my Grandma and my Momma lived in the kitchen, correcting each other's recipes as each created their own ethnic masterpieces. And, despite their individual desires to take their culinary secrets to the grave, they fessed all their secret formulas to Jane and me. Enjoy!

Steve

My family was ethnically neutral. My Mother's Mother, Grandma Minnie was a German Jew. She spoke German rather than Yiddish. And she was not a cook. The only food item that I remember from her was "The Butterfly Cake" which she carried on the train from Cake Masters in Manhattan. It was composed of two round sponge cakes; one of which was cut in half and placed on top of the bottom layer which was covered with whipped cream and a candied cherry which my sister & I fought over. (Even now, 50 years later, I still salivate.)

My Father's Mother was an Orthodox Jew who was a terrific cook. However, she came from England and her Jewish dishes were more British than Jewish. Many of her greatest culinary surprises used parts of the animal that the butcher threw out. Instead of chopped liver, we would get chopped kidneys. Needless to say, my early gastronomic experiences were not particularly mouth watering...except for The Butterfly Cake.

Jane

HOLIDAY COOKBOOK

Whether it's Christmas or Hanukkah, Easter or Passover; Jane has designed each dish to bring out the flavors of the originals without any of the greases and oils that your tummy tolerated years ago but your gall bladder says "NO" to today!

(Thanks to Momma's cooking, my gall bladder was removed in 1975)

Steve

Compiled Tested Edited

Jane Evers

Steve's Holiday Memories from Childhood

We celebrated both Chanukah AND Christmas. Christmas was great for most kids. You got off from school, Christmas parades, and eight thousand presents under the tree. Chanukah.. sucked..... at least for me. My cousins would run down Christmas morning to see a tree full of presents....big ones: toys, ponies, keys for a new car on the driveway, TVs that fell off Uncle Paulie's truck. We only got flat stuff.....Sweaters, books and galoshes.

Remember Galoshes? Those giant rubber boots with fifty buckles that you had to bend over and clip one at a time? I hated that. You see I was husky back then....So I'd bend over, close all fifty buckles stand up and black out. If I complained, I got lectured on what an ingrate I was and how bad things were in the old days in Europe.

Mom would ask me if I knew how many children in Europe had no shoes? Dad would counter with..." Eight people in the same apartment with one toilet.... in the hall---in another building..... We made toys from chicken bones.... We had nothing! But....come the holidays...we were grateful for everything we didn't have." My mother would finish with, "....and we were so poor we had to move in with a homeless family!"
Table of Contents

Table of Contents

My Mother's Italian Holiday Recipes

Soup

Entrees

Vegetables

Pasta & Starches

Dessert

Table of Contents

My Father's Jewish Holiday Recipes

Soup

Entrees

Starch

Vegetables

Dessert

I do remember Grandma Ida's potato latkes- a holiday specialty. They consisted of: grated potatoes, grated onions, enough salt to give a stroke to an elephant, shaped into a patty and deep fried in chicken fat.

There wasn't a person in Pop's family who ever needed stool softeners. After that dinner, most of them were afraid to cough!

Ah....I remember those days.........so does my cardiologist.

Italian Holidays

Christmas

First you should know that while Christmas is a family oriented holiday, Italians usually celebrate the New Year with friends rather than with family. There is even a saying that refers to this practice: "*Natale con i tuoi, Capodanno con chi vuoi,*" which means "Christmas with your family, New Year's with who you like."

In our times, when speaking of Christmas we refer to it as a period which goes from December 24th to January 6th and therefore includes Christmas Eve (December 24th), Christmas (December 25th), Saint Stephen (December 26th), New Year (night of December 31st - January 1st) and Epiphany (January 6th), that is represented by a likeable old lady, who, in the night between January 5th and 6th, enters the houses riding a broom, bringing presents and filling socks with candies for the kids who behaved well and coal for the ones who behaved like rascals.

During the period preceding the real holydays it is a tradition to set up the "Presepe" (Crib) and the Christmas tree. The "Presepe" (Crib) is the exact reproduction, by means of small statues, of scenes regarding Jesus' birth, while the tree is a fir, real or fake, decorated with colored balls and multicolored lights. Always as a tradition the "Presepe" (Crib) and the tree are set up on December 8th , the day of the Immacolata (the day the Virgin Mary is celebrated) and put away in the evening of next year on January 6th.

On the night of Saint Sylvester (San Silvestro), December 31st, a worldwide party crosses countries and time zones. In general, Italians celebrate like most others in the world often gathering to watch fireworks or setting off some of their own.

Easter

This is the most important Catholic religious celebration and it is meant to remember the resurrection of Jesus Christ. The observance of Easter usually lasts the entire weekend, starting with Thursday night, which would have been the night of Jesus' arrest. Holy or Good Friday is the day that commemorates Jesus' crucifixion, Saturday is spent in mourning with no festivities or fancy food allowed, and Sunday is the day for the celebration of the resurrection. Bells peal throughout Italy on Easter Sunday to mark the event. Easter Monday is also an official holiday in Italy.

Thanksgiving

Every family of Italian heritage has different culinary traditions to celebrate this holiday. An Italian Thanksgiving dinner might include ravioli con la zucca (pumpkin ravioli), tacchinella alla melagrana (roast turkey basted with pomegranate sauce and served with a pomegranate-and-giblet gravy), sweet Italian turkey sausage and mozzarella stuffing, baked sweet potatoes with lime and ginger, and even Italian cakes and pastries. What matters most, though, during *La Festa del Ringraziamento* isn't what ingredients are used, or who won the football game, but the opportunity for families and communities to come together and celebrate the season in a tradition that's timeless.

New Years Day

The annual rite of consuming good luck food for New Year's Day is observed all over the world. In Italy, lentils are eaten as a symbol of good luck and prosperity because they resemble tiny coins. Tuscans eat lentils with "Cotechino", a large pork sausage. People in Bologna and Modena eat lentils with "Zampone", the same sausage mixture stuffed into the skin of a pig's foot. In the Piedmont, little grains of rice symbolize money, so New Year's Day menus feature risotto and for added luck, a plate of beef or chicken would be served with spinach and lentils.

A Tree for Christmas

I was admiring the Christmas trees displayed in the store windows. I asked my Dad, 'Daddy, can we have a Hanukkah Tree?'

'What? No, of course not.' said Pop.

'Why not?' I asked again.

Bewildered, my Dad said, 'Well, Son, because the last time we had dealings with a lighted bush we spent 40 years in the wilderness.'

Italian Holiday Soups

Roasted Pumpkin & Pear Soup (Thanksgiving)

Tortellini in Brodo (Tortellini in Broth)
(Christmas Day or New Year's Eve)

Spring Milanese Minestrone Soup (Easter)

Roasted Pumpkin and Pear Soup

Thanksgiving

Oven at 375 degrees and Top of Stove cooking

Serves 6

Ingredients

3 small onions, peeled and diced

3 tablespoons butter

3 cloves garlic, peeled and minced

2 small pears, peeled, cored, roasted & coarsely chopped

4 cups roasted pumpkin flesh

Salt & pepper

4+ cups chicken broth (approximate)

½ teaspoon cinnamon

1. Preheat oven to 375 degrees.
2. Cut pumpkin into thick slices removing seeds and stringy loose flesh. Reserve the seeds for roasting.
3. Peel and core pears & cut in half
4. Line a baking sheet with aluminum foil and place pumpkin with pears on top.
5. Bake until pears (about 25 minutes) and pumpkin (about 45 minutes) are fork tender and beginning to brown.
6. Cool and scoop out pumpkin flesh keeping about 4 cups for the soup. Reserve the rest for another use (pumpkin bread is great).
7. Chop the pears coarsely.
8. In a heavy pot, heat the butter and add the onions.
9. Cook over medium low heat until the onions are translucent and beginning to brown. Add garlic and cook additional couple of minutes.
10. Add pears and pumpkin and about 4 cups of broth. Season with salt, pepper & cinnamon and cook over low heat for about 30 minutes.

11. Blend (I use a hand immersion blender), then taste and adjust seasonings or add more broth if too thick.
12. Serve soup warm with toasted pumpkin seeds or with your garnish of choice (sour cream, diced pears, shopped roasted chestnuts, fresh chopped watercress).

To roast pumpkin seeds:

Clean seeds. Pat dry. Toss seeds with 2 tablespoons olive oil, salt and pepper and place on a foil lined baking sheet. Roast in a preheated 375 degree oven for 7 to 10 minutes until seeds are lightly brown and crispy. Cool.

Tortellini in Brodo (Tortellini in Broth)

Christmas Day or New Year's Eve

Stovetop

(Serves 4-6)

Ingredients

Beef broth (If in a rush, you can use store bought)

1 celery rib, including leaves, cut into 3 pieces

1 medium carrot, peeled, cut into pieces

1 medium onion, peeled

3 chicken drumsticks

2 pieces beef shank with bones

6 beef bones with marrow

7 cups water

1 small piece Parmesan cheese rind

About 2 tablespoons salt

1 package fresh tortellini

Fresh parsley

1. Put all ingredients, except salt, in stockpot.
2. Cover with 3-½ quarts of cold water. Bring to a boil over high heat. Skim foam and fat that rises to the surface.
3. Add salt, cover, and simmer for 2-½ hours. Skim occasionally. Taste and adjust salt.
4. Pour through a fine mesh strainer into a large container.
5. Cool to room temperature, cover and refrigerate overnight.
6. The next day, skim off any excess fat that has accumulated on the surface.
7. Place broth back in saucepan and bring to simmer
8. Add tortellini and cook until tender (8 – 10 minutes). The tortellini will rise to the surface. Serve immediately. Garnish with chopped fresh parsley

Spring Milanese Minestrone Soup

Easter

Top of stove

Serves 6 to 8

Shopping List:
- Zucchini
- Green beans
- Baby spinach
- Arborio rice
- Fresh basil

Ingredients

2 medium zucchini, stems removed, halved lengthwise and cut into 1 inch pieces

1 large onion, peeled, cut into 1 inch thick rings, then 1 inch chunks

4 carrots, peeled, cut in half lengthwise then cut into 1 inch chunks

3 stalks celery, cut into 1 inch pieces

2 medium potatoes, peeled, cut into 1 inch pieces

4 ounces thin green beans, cut into 1 inch pieces

6 large plum tomatoes, halved, cored, gently squeezed to remove most seeds and cut into 1 inch pieces

8 ounces baby spinach leaves

4 tablespoons olive oil

Salt & pepper

7 to 8 cups broth (chicken, beef or vegetable)

4 ounces Italian rice (Arborio)

¼ cup basil leaves, freshly chopped

Freshly grated parmesan cheese

1. Heat the olive oil in a large stockpot. Add onion, carrots, celery and zucchini and cook 3 to 4 minutes
2. Add the beans and potatoes and cook an additional 3 minutes.
3. Add tomatoes and add 6 cups of broth. The vegetables should be covered with the broth coming about one inch above the vegetables in the pot.
4. Season lightly with salt and pepper and cover. Reduce heat to a simmer.

Continued on next page...

5. Cook for about 2 hours adding additional broth as needed.
6. Add spinach and rice and cook another 20 to 30 minutes or until the rice is just tender to the bite.
7. Stir in the chopped basil, adjust seasoning and allow to come to room temperature.
8. Serve with a drizzle of olive oil, cracked black pepper and grated cheese, if desired.

Mystery Soup

Anthropologists universally agree... The primary instinct for the survival of the species is reproduction! Except in my Momma's family. In Momma's family....you survive because you eat! And eat we did. Strangely enough I never remember leftovers; I do remember soup. Momma and Grandma Angelina's soup always had a familiar taste—a taste not unlike the taste of yesterday's entree. It wasn't as if we had any say in the matter---SPEAK WHEN YOU'RE SPOKEN TO!

Momma and Grandma would gather all the scraps from yesterday's feast throw them in a pot with an assortment of brown things found in a Tupperware container in the rear of the fridge...you know, next to that bottle with a half inch of ketchup in it. They'd mix it up, toss in anything, cook it for 24 hours add a pinch of this a pinch of that and voila!..................................soup.

Yeah there were bones and mystery crunchies mixed in but who cared? That soup with a loaf of Momma's garlic bread—heaven. I once found a hard red lump in the soup.....Poppa said it was dried tomato....I KNOW it was a lego.

Italian Holiday Entrees

Baked Stuffed Shrimp (New Year's Day)

Roasted Leg of Lamb (Easter)

Sausage Stuffed Turkey Roast (Thanksgiving)

People always ask me which holiday I liked best, Christmas or Hanukkah???

I know what I liked WORST about those holidays—CABOZELL and PTCHA. (no...it's spelled correctly)

Cabozelle is the Italian specialty Aunt Millie made for Christmas dinner. It is, in essence, roasted sheep's head (sans hair—avec eyes). Some kids are afraid of ghosts, heights, spiders. I was afraid of Cabozelle. AKA fear of food?

I think it's not unlike a small child seeing a clown for the first time; it works two ways: 1. The child laughs...or 2. The child screams, fills his diaper and even the sight of Clarabelle sends shivers through him for the rest of his life.

I was five when I had my first experience with Cabozelle—Uncle Frankie was ruthless. We had all sat down to Christmas dinner when Aunt Millie brought out a giant, silver dome covered, platter. I had no idea what was underneath the dome. Uncle Frankie moved that platter in front of me and told me to close my eyes for the big surprise. I complied. Uncle Frankie the removed the silver dome and told me to open my eyes. I did. Inches away from me was a giant, bloody skinned sheep's head—its eyes were open and it was staring straight at me. I started to vibrate, began to scream and slid off my booster chair. I remained under Aunt Millie's table till sometime after New Years.

To this day I have trouble bringing my grandkids to a petting zoo. I keep seeing those sheep without skin! They would stare at me—they knew—they knew. I also keep seeing Uncle Frankie, diving into that so-called feast and gingerly popping out the sheep's eye with his fork and dropping it into his mouth.

He would scare me into being good...he told me he's the one who ate Sammy Davis Jr's eye!

Baked Stuffed Shrimp

Christmas Eve

Steve top and over baking at 375 degrees

Serves 6

Ingredients For stuffing

1 cup chopped mushrooms (about ¼ pound)

3 tablespoons minced onion

2 tablespoons minced celery ribs

1 tablespoon minced garlic (about 3 cloves)

3 tablespoons finely chopped fresh parsley leaves

3 tablespoons unsalted butter

½ pound scallops, chopped, or lump crabmeat, picked over

½ cup chicken broth

32 Ritz crackers (about two thirds of a 12-ounce package), crushed into coarse crumbs

Ingredients For Shrimp

18 jumbo shrimp (about 2 pounds), shelled, leaving tail and connecting shell segment intact

2 tablespoons unsalted butter

¼ teaspoon paprika

Chopped fresh parsley leaves

Lemon wedges

1. Preheat oven to 375°F and butter a large baking dish.
2. In a large heavy skillet cook mushrooms, onion, celery, garlic, and parsley in butter over moderate heat, stirring occasionally, until softened and liquid mushrooms give off is evaporated.
3. Add scallops or crabmeat and cook over moderately high heat, stirring, 3 minutes.
4. Stir in broth and cracker crumbs and remove skillet from heat.
5. Butterfly shrimp by cutting lengthwise along inside curve, almost completely through. Split open shrimp and devein.

6. Mound about 2 tablespoons stuffing onto each shrimp, pressing gently, and put shrimp, stuffed sides up, in baking dish.
7. Melt butter and drizzle over shrimp. Sprinkle shrimp with paprika and bake 20 minutes, or until stuffing is golden.
8. Garnish shrimp with parsley and serve with lemon wedges.

Roasted Leg of Lamb

Easter

Oven at 375 degrees

Serves 4-6

Ingredients

6 oil packed anchovy fillets, drained and blotted with paper towels

3 large whole garlic cloves, peeled

2 tablespoons fresh thyme

2 tablespoons fresh rosemary leaves

Finely grated zest of 1 orange

¼ cup extra virgin olive oil

Salt and freshly ground pepper

1 small bone-in leg of lamb (about 5 pounds without the bone)

1 large yellow onion, coarsely chopped

1 large rib celery, trimmed and cut into 1 inch pieces

1 large carrot, peeled and chopped

2 cups dry white wine

1. Preheat the oven to 375.
2. In a food processor, combine the anchovies, garlic, thyme and rosemary.
3. Using a small paring knife, make 1 ½ inch deep slits all over the lamb. Spread the herb paste all over the lamb, working it into the slits; season the lamb with salt and pepper.
4. Using seven or eight long pieces of kitchen string, tie the roast at 1 inch intervals.
5. Scatter the onion, carrot and celery in the bottom of a roasting pan just large enough to hold the lamb and lay the meat on top.
6. Roast for 1 hour 40 minutes to 2 hours until an instant-read thermometer, inserted in the center of the thickest part of the meat, registered 140 degrees to 145 degrees. For medium-rare, cook to 135 degrees.

7. Transfer the lamb to a cutting board, tent it loosely with aluminum foil and let rest for 20 minutes.
8. Meanwhile, set the roasting pan over high heat.
9. Pour in the wine and bring the liquid to a boil, scraping up any browned bits from the bottom of the pan.
10. Strain it into a small sauce pan, pressing on the vegetables to extract as much liquid as possible. Discard the vegetables.
11. Skim the fat from the surface and boil until the sauce is reduced to 1 cup, about 20 minutes, then pour it into a gravy boat.
12. Remove the kitchen string from the lamb and cut the meat across the grain into thin slices.
13. Serve at once with the sauce.

Sausage Stuffed Turkey Roast

Thanksgiving

Stove top cooking and Oven at 375 degrees

Serves 6

This is a great stuffing that is carb-free (no bread)

Ingredients

4 pound turkey breast, boned

Salt and pepper

1 (10 ounce) package fresh spinach

1 small onion, finely diced

4 tablespoons olive oil

2 cloves garlic, minced

Salt & pepper to taste

¾ pound sweet Italian sausage

½ cup dried cranberries

3 teaspoons crushed fennel seeds

1 ½ cups chicken or turkey broth

½ cup dry white wine

2 tablespoons flour

1. Heat 2 tablespoons of oil and sauté the onions until they are tender.
2. Add garlic and cook until sizzling.
3. Remove onions and garlic and place in bowl.
4. If using baby spinach, use whole leaf. Otherwise remove thick stem and veins from larger leaves. Either steam or microwave the spinach until wilted.
5. Squeeze to remove all excess liquid and coarsely chop. Add to the onions and garlic.
6. Remove sausage meat from the casings and crumble into the bowl with the spinach and onions.
7. Add salt and pepper, half the fennel and the dried cranberries and mix well.

8. Preheat the oven to 375 degrees.
9. Butterfly the breast and lay flat open, pounding with a meat mallet to create even thickness throughout.
10. Spread the spinach mixture across the breast, leaving ½ inch border all around.
11. Roll up tightly and tie with kitchen twine.
12. Place into a small roasting pan and rub the surface with the remaining oil and season with salt, pepper and remaining fennel seeds
13. Mix together the chicken broth and white wine.
14. Roast in the preheated oven for about 1 hour 20 minutes or until internal temperature reaches 150 degrees basting every 15 minutes with the broth and wine mixture.
15. Remove the breast roll from the pan and cover with a tent of foil.
16. To make gravy, remove excess oil from pan and set on stove top adding the remaining white wine broth mixture.
17. Scrape up all the browned bit from the bottom and cook until it has reduced by half. Remove a few spoonfuls of broth to a separate cup and mix the flour into the broth. Then mix into the gravy.
18. Season with salt and pepper and strain to remove any bits.
19. Cut off the twine around the turkey and slice into ½ inch slices and arrange on platter
20. Serve, offering the sauce or gravy on the side.

CHRISTMAS COOKING

Italians start cooking for Christmas right after Thanksgiving. Momma would get together with Aunt Millie. Aunt Millie's kitchen was loaded with every pot they had. Even things that weren't quite pots were used: Pails, wheel barrows—if it could hold water, it was drafted into service. The creation of "Sauce" or as they called it...Gravy, was an art unto itself. By 7:00 AM two 55 gallon drums of sauce were bubbling away on the stove. Nobody could say a word to either Momma or Aunt Millie as they worked with the fluidity of a finely tuned operating room staff. They cooked by smell. They'd sniff.... "It need a little more this.... a little that...." Italian culinary bloodhounds. Everybody walked around the house with fogged glasses. Time was of the essence as the feeding frenzy would start by noon.

Smells permeated the kitchen, house...neighborhood—mostly garlic, oregano and cheese. The main dishes were composed of: Spaghetti, Cooked eel—fresh killed by my Momma (I won't go into the details of the eel slaughter but after watching one such slaying....I'm still afraid of my Mother!) Roast ham, Veal, Cabozelle, pig balls, horse's lips??? Who knew? It was meat smothered in sauce—any meat smothered in sauce.

By the time the main dishes were served, most of the guests were too tipsy from the "Vino" to know, or care what they were eating; they just kept shaking hot peppers on everything to give it some taste.

Italian Holiday Vegetables

Artichoke Gratinata (New Year's Day)

Sweet & Sour Roasted Beets & Onions (Easter)

Roman Green Beans with Peppery Oil & Garlic (Thanksgiving)

Artichoke Gratinata

New Year's Day

Stove top & oven at 450 degrees

Serves 4

Ingredients

3 tablespoons olive oil

1 garlic clove, minced

1 pound frozen artichoke hearts, thawed

2 tablespoons chopped fresh parsley leaves

¾ teaspoon salt

¼ teaspoon freshly ground black pepper

⅛ teaspoon red pepper flakes

½ cup chicken broth

¼ cup Marsala wine

2 tablespoons butter

⅓ cup plain bread crumbs

⅓ cup grated parmesan cheese

1. Preheat oven to 450 degrees
2. Warm the olive oil in a heavy skillet over medium high heat.
3. Add garlic and cook for 1 minute.
4. Add artichoke hearts, parsley, salt, pepper and red pepper flakes and cook until artichoke hearts are starting to brown at the edges (about 3 minutes).
5. Add the chicken broth and wine and simmer for 3 minutes.
6. Transfer the artichoke mixture to a 2-quart baking dish greased with cooking spray.
7. Melt the butter in the same skillet used to cook artichokes.
8. In a small bowl mix the melted butter with the bread crumbs.
9. Stir in the parmesan cheese and top the artichokes with the bread crumbs.
10. Bake until the top is golden (about 10 minutes).

Sweet and Sour Roasted Beets and Onions

Thanksgiving
Oven at 365 degrees
Serves 4

Ingredients

6 medium beets
2 medium red onions (leave whole with skins on)

Dressing

⅓ cup olive oil
2 tablespoons red wine vinegar
1 tablespoon honey
2 teaspoons capers
Salt & pepper (to taste)
¼ cup freshly chopped parsley

1. Preheat oven to 365 degrees.
2. Wash the beets and place beets and onions in a casserole dish.
3. Cover and bake until fork tender about 1 to 1 ½ hours. Cool.
4. Peel the beets and cut into ½ inch wide strips.
5. Peel the onions and cut into ⅓ inch slices.
6. Mix together the beets and onions in a serving bowl.
7. Mix the dressing in a separate bowl until well blended.
8. Pour the dressing onto the beets until mixed.
9. Serve at room temperature.

Roman Green Beans with Peppery Oil and Garlic

Thanksgiving

Stove top cooking

Serves 4 to 6

Ingredients

1 pound Romano Beans (also known as pole beans), trimmed and cut in half, if long

3 tablespoons olive oil

2 cloves freshly peeled garlic, minced

1 teaspoon freshly chopped oregano

¼ to ½ teaspoon freshly ground pepper

Dash of sea salt

½ fresh red chili pepper, minced (optional)

1 teaspoon grated lemon rind

2 tablespoons freshly squeezed lemon juice

1. Bring a pot of salted water to boil and drop in beans.
2. Cook for about 4 to 5 minutes or until just tender crisp. Drain & set aside.
3. In the same pot, heat the olive oil and add the garlic and cook until just sizzling.
4. Add the remaining ingredients to the oil & stir.
5. Add the beans back into the pot and toss until they are coated with the flavored oil.
6. Serve immediately.

THANKSGIVING

Thanksgiving was a mixed bag of ethnicity. Although the holiday had its roots in Christian tradition, in the US, it melded into acceptance by most religions and it became, essentially, a celebration of generic....thanks.

If Momma held Thanksgiving, due to the size of her dining room, Thanksgiving took place in most rooms of the house. The children's table was in the basement—I sat at the children's table till I was 55 and, at 55, I was the youngest at the children's table.

The standard fare was: Ham with cloves-- I HATE CLOVES and Turkey. The ecumenical cooks shared the kitchen adding their cultural flavors to each dish. Momma once attempted to put oregano on Bubie's (Daddy's Mom) sweet potato pudding. Bubie wrestled it out of Momma's hand and threatened her with a meat cleaver.

I liked turkey skin—I LOVED turkey skin. At that age, I could eat 5 pounds of turkey skin. Mamma said, "Stop...it's a no good a fa you!" I didn't listen... They took my gall bladder out when I was 8.

Italian Holiday Pastas & Starches

Baked Ziti (Easter)

Linguine with Clam Sauce (Christmas Eve)

Rosemary Garlic Roasted Potatoes (Easter)

Baked Ziti

Easter

Stove top cooking and oven baking at 400 degrees

Serves 6

Ingredients For Sauce

2 tablespoons olive oil

2 tablespoons onions, minced

2 cloves garlic, minced

1 carrot, peeled and finely diced

1 celery stalk, finely diced

4 link hot sausage (or sweet if you prefer)

Salt & pepper

1 teaspoon dried oregano

¼ cup fresh parsley, finely chopped

½ cup red wine

2 (14 ounce) cans chopped tomatoes

Ingredients For Pasta

1 pound of ziti (or other dried pasta)

1 ½ cups diced mozzarella or fontina cheese

3 ounces parmesan, freshly grated

3 beaten eggs

1. Brown sausage links well in heavy saucepan. Remove and cut into ½ inch rounds.
2. Heat oil in same saucepan and cook vegetables until softened (about 7 – 10 minutes).
3. Add wine and cook until reduced by half.
4. Add tomatoes, salt, pepper, oregano, sausage pieces and parsley and simmer 60 minutes until thickened.
5. Preheat oven to 400 degrees.
6. Meanwhile, cook pasta until al dente.

7. Drain pasta and add to the sauce, mixing well.
8. In a buttered, ovenproof dish place ⅓ of pasta & sauce, then sprinkle with ⅓ of diced cheese.
9. Repeat these layers twice more.
10. Pour the beaten eggs over pasta and then sprinkle with grated cheese.
11. Bake in preheated 400 degree oven until bubbly.
12. Let stand 5 minutes before serving.

Linguine with Clam Sauce

Christmas Eve

Stove top cooking

Serves 4 – main course or 8 first course

Ingredients

⅓ cup extra virgin olive oil

1 medium onion, chopped

6 garlic cloves, peeled and finely chopped

¾ teaspoon dried hot red pepper flakes

¼ teaspoon dried oregano

⅓ cup dry white wine

⅓ cup bottled clam juice

1 pound linguine

2 pounds small cockles (clams) up to one-inch across – 5 to 6 dozen, scrubbed well

2 tablespoons cold unsalted butter, cut in small pieces

⅓ cup fresh flat-leaf parsley, chopped

1. Heat oil in a 5 to 6 quart heavy pot over medium high heat until hot, but not smoking.
2. Sauté onion, stirring until golden about 4 minutes.
3. Add garlic, red pepper flakes and oregano and cook, stirring occasionally, until garlic is golden, about 2 minutes.
4. Stir in wine and clam juice and boil, uncovered, stirring occasionally, until slightly reduced, about 3 minutes.
5. Cook pasta in a 6 to 8 quart pot of boiling salted water until al dente, then drain in a colander.
6. While pasta is cooking, stir cockles into sauce and simmer, covered, stirring occasionally, until cockles open wide, about 4 to 6 minutes. (Discard any cockles that have not opened after 6 minutes.)
7. Remove pot from heat and stir in butter until melted.
8. Add pasta to sauce along with parsley and salt to taste, then toss with sauce until well combined.

Rosemary Garlic Roasted Potatoes

Easter

Oven at 400 degrees

Serves 6

Ingredients

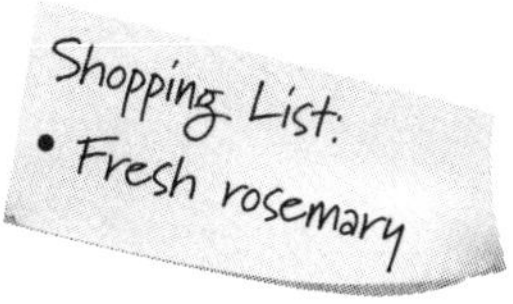

2 pounds potatoes

3 cloves garlic, peeled and cut into 3 pieces

4 tablespoons fresh rosemary, chopped

5 tablespoons olive oil

Salt & pepper

1. Preheat the oven to 400 degrees
2. In an ovenproof casserole dish, mix together all of the listed ingredients
3. Cook for about 45 minutes or until potatoes are soft when pierced with a fork and beginning to brown.
4. Serve hot.

Chocolate

I'm allergic to chocolate. I loved chocolate as a kid. It was the cheap after dinner, after lunch, after breakfast, during breakfast, after school and pre-dinner treat. Whether it was Ovaltine, Hershey's chunky bar or Grandma Ida's homemade fudge, Grandma Angelina's chocolate cake, Momma's chocolate cookies, chocolate was the treat of choice for me and the family. Sounds good right? I was so allergic to chocolate I used to get migraine headaches from chocolate---at the age of three!

Mom and Pop would take me to pediatrician after pediatrician searching for brain damage or the like...all to no avail. No one thought of food allergies back then. If you were allergic to something you were "defective" and labeled as a pariah in the family group.

My sister (six years older) put two and two together. She also got headaches from chocolate AND pimples; so her Doctor told her to stay away from chocolate because of the pimples. When she cut out the chocolate; the headaches disappeared. My family, not willing to acknowledge that their food might have caused our suffering, attributed our miraculous cure to Grandma's prayers to St. Nestle.

Italian Holiday Desserts

Biancomangiare
(Almond Clouds in Vanilla Almond Milk) (Easter)

Christmas Cookies (Christmas)

Easiest Chocolate Mousse (New Year's Day)

Breads Italian vs. Jewish

Italian Bread: thick crispy, bullet-proof crust on the outside. Soft but slightly chewy on the inside. Best bought at an Italian bakery. Sliced open and toasted in the oven with garlic and butter. TO DIE FOR

Challah: (AKA egg bread) Thin braided, lightly egg yolk basted, crispy crust on the outside. Soft—never chewy on the inside. Best when grandma makes it....Unless it's grandma Angelina who constantly forgets to put the eggs in Challah, forgets to baste it, forgets to braid it, overcooks it, adds caraway seeds--- bad Wonderbread at best.

Grandma Angelina is convinced that all good breads have to have loud crunching sounds associated with eating them. No bias here! Noisy foods are better than silent foods...ask grandma.

Come to think of it... for the perfect "silent" Challah; pick one up at the supermarket.

Biancomangiare –
Almond Clouds in Vanilla Almond Milk

Easter
Top of stove
Serves 8

Ingredients

1 ½ envelopes unflavored gelatin
½ pound blanched almonds
6 ½ cups whole milk
Zest of 2 lemons
2 cups sugar
2 tablespoons almond oil (not extract)
1 cup heavy cream, very cold
1 tablespoon vanilla extract
1 egg plus 4 egg yolks
Seeds from 1 pomegranate

1. Place the gelatin in 2 cups of cold water and set aside.
2. Place almonds in a food processor and grind to a powder.
3. Combine rest of milk and lemon zest in a nonreactive saucepan (glass). Add the ground almonds and bring to a boil over medium-high heat.
4. Remove from heat, cover and let stand 20 minutes.
5. Line a sieve with cheesecloth and strain milk mixture, pressing with the back of a spoon to remove all of the liquid. Discard the solids.
6. Set aside 1 ½ cups of the flavored milk for the sauce and place the remaining milk, 1 ½ cups sugar and the soaked gelatin in a saucepan.
7. Bring just to a boil, stirring constantly. Remove from heat immediately and allow to cool to room temperature.
8. Grease 10 6-ounce ramekins with almond oil and set aside.

9. Whip the cream to soft peaks and fold the cooled almond milk and vanilla into the whipped cream.
10. Spoon the mixture into the greased molds up to 90% full and refrigerate for at least 4 hours.
11. Meanwhile, beat together the egg and egg yolks. Add to the reserved flavored milk and add remaining ½ cup sugar.
12. Place over medium heat, stirring constantly to a high simmer (175 degrees).
13. Remove from heat, pour through a strainer into a small bowl and refrigerate 1 hour.
14. To serve, unmold ramekins. You may need to tip bottoms in hot water to release. Run a sharp knife around the edges and unmold on plates.
15. Whisk the sauce to loosen it and pour over the custard. Garnish with pomegranate seeds.

Christmas Cookies

Christmas
Oven baking at 350 degrees
Serves lots – 8 ½ dozen

Ingredients

1 cup butter, softened
2 cups sugar
3 eggs
1 carton (15 ounces) ricotta cheese
2 teaspoons vanilla extract
4 cups all-purpose flour
1 teaspoon salt
1 teaspoon baking soda

Frosting

¼ cup butter, softened
3 to 4 cups confectioners' sugar
½ teaspoon vanilla extract
3 to 4 tablespoons milk
Colored sprinkles

1. In a large bowl, cream butter & sugar.
2. Add eggs, one at a time, beating well after each addition.
3. Beat in ricotta and vanilla.
4. Combine flour, salt and baking soda in another bowl.
5. Gradually add flour mixture to creamed mixture.
6. Drop by rounded teaspoonfuls 2 inches apart onto greased baking sheets
7. Bake at 350 degrees for 10 to 12 minutes or until lightly browned. Remove to wire racks to cool.
8. In a bowl, cream butter, sugar and vanilla. Add enough milk until frosting reaches spreading consistency.
9. Frost cooled cookies and immediately decorate with sprinkles.
10. Store in refrigerator.

Easiest Chocolate Mousse

New Years Day

Top of stove

Serves 4

Ingredients

½ cup whole milk

1 to 2 tablespoons sugar (3 tablespoons if no liqueur is added)

2 tablespoons of flavored liqueur choice (amaretto, chocolate, coffee, orange etc.)

1 cup bittersweet chocolate, finely chopped (or chocolate chips)

3 extra large eggs whites

Whipped cream

Garnishes (crumbles of amaretti cookies, candied orange, chocolate covered coffee bean etc.)

1. In a small saucepan, heat the milk with the sugar and liqueur (if using) until it is hot and the sugar has dissolved. Do not allow to boil.
2. Place the chocolate in a blender and pour the hot milk over top.
3. Run the blender until the chocolate has melted, about a minute.
4. Add the egg whites and blend on high until very light, about another minute.
5. Pour the mousse into individual cups and refrigerate at least 3 to 4 hours.
6. Serve with a dollop of whipped cream on top and garnish with ingredients of your choice.

Note: This recipe can easily be doubled, but be aware that the blender needs to be able to accommodate all the liquid.

Jewish Holidays – what they're all about

Rosh Hashanah

Rosh Hashanah literally means "Head of the Year". It is the celebration of the Jewish New Year, observed on the first day of the Hebrew month of Tishrei, usually in September or October.

Rosh Hashanah marks the beginning of a ten-day period of prayer, self-examination and repentance, culminating on the fast day of Yom Kippur. Special customs observed on Rosh Hashanah include; the sounding of the shofar, using round challah, eating apples and honey (and other sweet foods) which symbolizes the hope for a sweet new year.

Yom Kippur

Yom Kippur is the "Day of Atonement". It is the annual Jewish observance of fasting, prayer and repentance. It is considered to be the holiest day in the Jewish calendar.

In three separate passages in the Torah, the Jewish people are told, "the tenth day of the seventh month is the Day of Atonement. It shall be a sacred occasion for you: You shall practice self-denial." (Leviticus 23:27). Fasting is seen as fulfilling this biblical commandment.

So observant Jews attend synagogue for the day and refrain from eating. Of course, there is a "break-the-fast" celebration where typically bagels, lox and sweets are consumed in great quantities.

Sukkoth

Sukkoth, is a Hebrew word meaning "booths" or "huts," and refers to the Jewish festival of giving thanks for the fall harvest, as well as the commemoration of the forty years of Jewish wandering in the desert after Sinai.

Sukkoth is celebrated five days after Yom Kippur on the 15th of Tishrei and is marked by several distinct traditions. One tradition, which takes the commandment to "dwell in booths" literally, is to build a *sukkah*, a booth or hut. A *sukkah* is often erected by Jews during this festival, and it is common practice for some to eat and even live in these temporary dwellings during Sukkoth.

Chanukah

Chanukah, meaning "dedication" in Hebrew, refers to the joyous eight-day celebration during which Jews commemorate the victory of the Macabees over the armies of Syria in 165 B.C.E. and the subsequent liberation and "re-dedication" of the Temple in Jerusalem.

The modern home celebration of Chanukah centers around the lighting of the *chanukiah*, a special menorah for Chanukah; unique foods, latkes and jelly doughnuts; and special songs and games.

Purim

Purim is celebrated by the reading of the Scroll of Esther, known in Hebrew as the *Megillat Esther*, which relates the basic story of Purim. Under the rule of King Ahashuerus, Haman, the King's prime minister, plots to exterminate all of the Jews of Persia. His plan is foiled by Queen Esther and her uncle Mordechai, who ultimately save the Jews of the land from destruction. The reading of the *megillah* is typically a rowdy affair, punctuated by booing and noise-making when Haman's name is read aloud.

The significance in Purim lies not so much in how it began, but in what it has become -a thankful and joyous affirmation of Jewish survival against all odds.

Passover

Pesach, known as Passover in English, is a major Jewish spring festival, commemorating the Exodus of the Jews from Egypt over 3,000 years ago. The ritual observance of this holiday centers around a special home service called the seder (meaning "order") and a festive meal; the prohibition of of *chametz* (leaven – anything that swells including rice, bread, corn & beans; and the eating of matzah (an unleavened bread).

On the eve of the fifteenth day of Nisan in the Hebrew calendar, we read from a book called the *hagaddah*, meaning "telling," which contains the order of prayers, rituals, readings and songs for the Pesach seder. The Pesach seder is the only ritual meal in the Jewish calendar year for which such an order is prescribed, hence its name.

Shavuot

Shavuot is a Hebrew word meaning "weeks" and refers to the Jewish festival marking the giving of the Torah at Mount Sinai. Shavuot, like so many other Jewish holidays, began as an ancient agricultural festival, marking the end of the spring barley harvest and the beginning of the summer wheat harvest. Shavuot was distinguished in ancient times by bringing crop offerings to the Temple in Jerusalem.

Special customs on Shavuot are the reading of the Book of Ruth, which reminds us that we too can find a continual source of blessing in our tradition. Traditionally, dairy dishes are served on this holiday to symbolize the sweetness of the Torah, as well as the "land of milk and honey".

Jewish Holiday Soups

Fresh Tomato Soup (Shavuot)

Leek, Carrot & Squash Soup (Passover)

Mitzapuny (meaty split pea, bean & barley soup) (Sukkoth)

Fresh Tomato Soup

Shavuot

Stove top cooking

Serves 4

Shopping List:
- Vegetable stock – Buy or make see recipe

Ingredients

2 tablespoons vegetable oil

1 onion, chopped into small dice

1 clove garlic, finely sliced

1 carrot, chopped into small dice

2 tablespoons tomato puree

2lb tomatoes (~8 medium), cut in quarter and cut out central hard core

4 sun dried tomatoes in oil, or soaked

1 teaspoon sugar or sugar substitute

1 bay leaf

4 cups vegetable stock*

Salt and pepper to taste

1. Prepare the vegetables
2. Heat the oil in a large saucepan and add the onion, carrot and garlic. Cook over a low heat, stirring occasionally until softened, about 10 minutes.
3. Add the tomato puree then the tomatoes; sun dried tomatoes, sugar and bay leaf.
4. Cover the saucepan and cook for about 10 minutes until the tomatoes are softened and cooked. Stir occasionally to make sure the tomatoes don't stick.
5. Pour in the stock, bring to the boil then turn the heat down and simmer for about 30 minutes.
6. Leave the soup to cool. When cool, remove the tomato skins and blend using a hand blender or liquidizer.
7. Reheat; add a little water or stock if the soup is too thick.
8. Taste and season as necessary.

Suggestions:

- To make the tomato soup into a creamy soup stir in 1 cup of cream or ½ and ½
- For a richer taste top with sour cream, yogurt or shredded cheese (mozzarella, cheddar or parmesan)

Homemade Vegetable Stock

Ingredients

2 leeks, clean, white and pale green parts only, cut into 1-inch rounds

2 carrots cut into 1 inch rounds

1 small onion, cut into 1-inch pieces

3 garlic cloves

8 cups water

5 flat-leaf parsley sprigs

2 thyme springs

1 dried bay leaf

2 teaspoons whole black pepper, crushed

1. In a medium saucepan, sprayed with cooking spray, cook leeks, carrots, onions and garlic covered, over medium heat, stirring occasionally for 10 minutes
2. Add water, parsley, thyme, bay leaf, and peppercorns.
3. Raise heat to high and bring to boil.
4. Reduce heat and simmer, uncovered, for 30 minutes.
5. Pour through a cheesecloth-lined strainer and discard any solids.

Matzo

AKA Jewish flat bread.

Matzo's typically a Passover food item. I know that the term "food item" seems rather cold and non-descript. It's like reading the package of some American cheeses-- "non-dairy, processed, cheesy food. Warning: May contain some ingredients that cause nutrition!"

Matzo is made, for the most part, of all natural ingredients. Nothing artificial and it never needs preservatives. Why: it never goes bad. It's like those 4000 year old honeys they find in the tombs-- still good. Scrape of the dust and spread it on a ritz.

Matzo comes in a two basic varieties: Dry and Extra dry. According to Talmudic Law; Matzo may never be eaten without something on it-- butter, jelly, chicken fat, KY jelly; substances which provide lubricating protection as you swallow.

There's a tradition on Passover where a Matzo is folded in a napkin and hidden somewhere in the house. It's then the job of the children at the table to search the house and find the Matzo. The first one to find the Matzo wins. Wins what? They usually win a dollar. Poppa was so cheap; if we found the Matzo, he'd let us keep it-- what an incentive! We all pretended to search. We never did.

Fourteen years later Mom and Pop sold the house; the new buyers found the hidden Matzo-- it was still good!

Leek, Carrot and Squash Soup

Passover

Stove top cooking

Serves 4 – 6

Ingredients

1-2 tablespoon canola or vegetable oil

1 onion, chopped

1 large leek, cleaned and cut in small pieces

4 carrots, peeled and cut into small pieces

1 medium butternut squash, peeled and cut into small pieces

6 cups vegetable stock (fresh or canned)

1 tablespoon honey

Salt and freshly ground pepper

1. Prepare the vegetables; chop the onion. Wash the leek and cut into small pieces. Peel the carrots and squash and cut into even sized small pieces.
2. Heat the oil in a large saucepan. Add the onion and leek and sauté for about 5 minutes until starting to soften.
3. Add the carrots and squash and sweat for 10-15minutes, stirring occasionally.
4. Add the stock and honey. Cook for about 40 minutes until vegetables are soft.
5. Blend using a liquidizer or stick blender.
6. Season to taste with salt and freshly ground black pepper.

Mitzapuny

(Meaty split pea, bean & barley soup)

Sukkoth

Top of stove

Serves 8 to 10

Ingredients

12 cups water

2 to 3 pounds soup beef, trimmed of all surface fat and cut into large chunks

3 small onions, peeled and left whole

4 to 6 medium carrots or about 1 pound peeled baby carrots, cut into ½ inch chunks

2 celery stalks, thinly sliced

1 ¼ cups dry green split peas, sorted and rinsed

1 cup dry baby lima beans, sorted and rinsed

½ cup uncooked pearly barley, rinsed

1 teaspoon salt

¼ teaspoon ground black (or white) pepper

1. Bring water to a boil in a 6-quart or larger soup pot over high heat.
2. Add meat and lower heat so water simmers. Gently cook the meat for 30 minutes, skimming off and discarding all the foam that rises to the surface.
3. Prepare remaining ingredients.
4. Add remaining ingredients, cover the pot and simmer soup, stirring occasionally for about 3 hours longer or until the split peas have disintegrated, the meat is very tender and the soup thick.
5. If too thick, stir in some water.
6. Remove and discard the onions before serving.
7. Adjust seasonings to taste.

Food...food...food

I was always the family mediator. After the mob (no pun intended) fed and drank—and the emphasis was on "drank." What, Jews don't drink you say???" Oh, they learn; trust me, they learn. The family would sit and laugh about how stuffed they were. They'd shout to Momma, "You did it again Marie.... I couldn't eat anther crumb....We're gonna explode!" The tables nodded, their stomachs growling in mutual agreement.

And then..."Uncle Charlie would start, "Now if Paulie was here..." Uncle Frankie joined in, "God bless Paulie...he don't need no family no more... business, business..."

I'd interject, "You know, he just started a new company and this is the first year...."

Momma interrupted, "Stevie! What, now my own son turns again his family!"

I said, "Mom, I'm not turning against....."

Uncle Frankie barked back, "Stevie... You calling your Momma a liar!"

"Dad," I pleaded, "Could you say something here in my defense?" My father looked up, dessert crumbs dropping off his chin... "Marie.....this is delicious. Son, as soon as I finish this, we'll talk..."

Uncle Charlie turned to my Dad and shouted, "Louie, where'd you get that?"

My Mom would then bring out the rest of the dessert: Cookies, Cannoles, Pies,, Zukoolies, Schvartoomoze, Farkulisko pudding, Marigrossos cake with double strouzzi filling. In an instant, everybody would forget about Uncle Paulie's digressions.

My life lesson? Never try to get between an Italian or Jew and his cake.

Jewish Holiday Entrees

Orange-Glazed Chicken Breasts (Passover)

Quick "Unstuffed" Sweet & Sour Cabbage & Beef (Sukkoth)

Sweet Soy Salmon
(Passover or "Break-the-fast" for Yom Kippur)

Orange-Glazed Chicken Breasts

Passover

Oven at 350 degrees

Serves 10

Ingredients

1 ½ cups matzo meal (or ground nuts for a gluten free diet)

3 tablespoons finely chopped fresh parsley

1 ½ teaspoons ground ginger

¾ teaspoon salt

¼ teaspoon ground black pepper

3 to 4 extra-large egg whites or 2 eggs or ½ cup pareve egg substitute

3 to 4 pounds boned and skinned chicken breasts (about 12)

1 (12 ounce) jar orange marmalade

1 cup white table wine (your choice)

3 tablespoons canola or safflower oil

1. Line one large or two smaller roasting pans with aluminum foil.
2. Spray with cooking oil.
3. Preheat oven to 350 degrees.
4. In a medium bowl, combine matzo meal, parsley, ginger, salt and pepper.
5. Put the egg whites into another bowl and lightly beat them until frothy.
6. Dip each chicken breast into egg white and then coat with the matzo meal mixture.
7. Arrange breasts in prepared pan(s) close together but don't overlap the breasts.
8. In a small saucepan or the microwave, put the marmalade, wine & oil and mix well.
9. Slowly bring the mixture to a brief boil.

10. Spoon the mixture over the chicken breasts so all tops are moistened and there are some orange slivers on each breast.
11. Bake at 350 degrees uncovered for 35 to 40 minutes.

Optional coating for chicken – because I don't eat any wheat products, I used ground almonds for the chicken breasts. It's a little more filling than the matzo coating, but very delicious.

Quick "Unstuffed" Sweet-and-Sour Cabbage and Beef

Sukkoth

Top of Stove

Serves 4 - 5

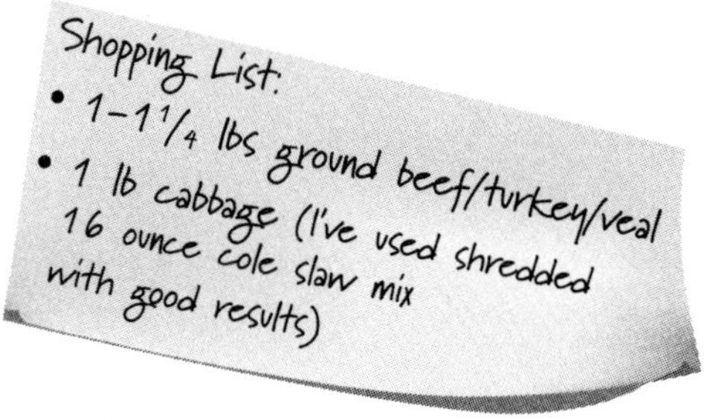

Ingredients

1 to 1 ¼ pounds either lean ground beef or turkey or veal

1 medium onion, finely chopped

1 (15 to 16 ounce) can plain tomato sauce

½ cup unsweetened applesauce

¼ cup water

5 tablespoons cider vinegar (to taste)

3 tablespoons packed dark brown sugar (to taste)

⅛ teaspoon ground black pepper

4 cups (about 1 pound) finely chopped green (white) cabbage

1 cup cooked rice (instant rice can be used)

1. In a 12-inch wide deep skillet or a Dutch oven, cook the ground meat and onion over medium heat.
2. Break up the meat as it is cooking.
3. When meat is brown and onion tender drain off all excess fat.
4. Add tomato sauce, applesauce, water, vinegar, brown sugar and pepper.
5. Bring mixture to boil and stir constantly. Mix in the cabbage which wilts as it cooks.
6. Lower the heat and simmer, covered, stirring occasionally for 25 to 30 minutes until cabbage is very tender.
7. Cook rice according to package instructions.
8. Stir in the cooked rice and heat until it is cooked through.
9. Serve in bowls.

Sweet Soy Salmon

Passover or "end-of-fast" breakfast

Oven at 350 degrees

Serves 4

This tasty sweet soy salmon is a wonderful appetizer and can also be served as a main dish, depending on the size of the salmon pieces. I prefer to use fillet of salmon rather than steaks, as there are no bones, but this would also work with steaks.

Don't cook the fish for too long – just until the white fat starts to ooze out of the salmon and it no longer looks raw.

Ingredients

4 Salmon pieces (steak or fillet)

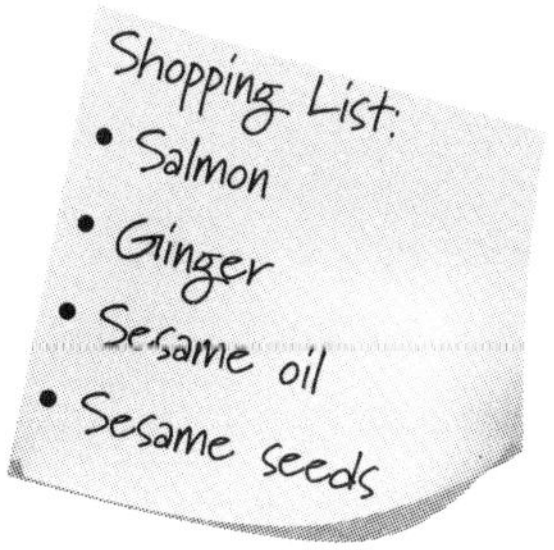

Marinade

4-8 tsp fresh grated ginger

4 cloves garlic, grated or crushed

8 tbsp soy sauce

8 tbsp honey

8 drops sesame oil

Sesame seeds

1. Mix the marinade ingredients together excluding the sesame seeds.
2. Put the salmon into the marinade and leave for an hour in the fridge.
3. When you are ready to bake, heat the oven to 350F and bake the salmon, covered for about 20 minutes. Check to see if it is cooked – do not overcook! The salmon should flake easily, and should have lost its raw look. It is much better to slightly undercook salmon than to overcook it.
4. Sprinkle with sesame seeds before serving.

PTCHA is usually served as a last meal

Let's now discuss PTCHA (no I didn't just clear my throat). To Poppa, Ptcha was the reward you get for working hard all year; a delicacy reserved for European blue-bloods. To the rest of the family, Ptcha was a bucket of animal scraps encased in a cold mucus-ee green jello. Here are some of the ingredients— you decide. The primary ingredient is ....Cow foot, the whole foot nothing but the foot (so help me God).

You place the foot in a pot, fill it with water and cook it for (this is true) 12–18 hours. Pull the meat off the bones, chop it, pour the gook in a pyrex dish, add spices and leave it in the fridge overnight. You know it's ready when it clots in the pyrex bowl.

Now I may be opinionated.... but just looking at this clump initiated my gag reflex. Mom proudly served it to Poppa with cooked noodles and an in-flight sickness bag.

In Europe, PTCHA is usually served to uncooperative death row prisoners as a last meal.

How many foods have driven you into therapy?

Jewish Holiday Starches

Cranberry-Pistachios Couscous (Shavuot)

Mushroom-Onion Farfel Kugel (Passover)

Crisp Fried Potato Latkes (Chanukah)

Cranberry Pistachios Couscous

Shavuot
Stove top cooking
Serves 4

Ingredients

1 ⅓ cups water
¾ cup couscous
⅛ cup pistachios, shelled and chopped
⅛ cup unsweetened coconut
¼ cup dried cranberries, chopped
dash of salt

1. Bring water to a boil, add couscous and salt; cover and remove from heat.
2. After 5 minutes, fluff the couscous with a fork and add the pistachios, unsweetened coconut, and dried cranberries.

Mushroom-Onion Farfel Kugel

Passover
Oven at 350 degree
Serves 12

Ingredients

3 tablespoons olive or canola oil
3 medium onions, finely chopped
2 garlic cloves, finely minced
4 celery stalks, thinly sliced
1 pound fresh mushrooms, cleaned and sliced (about 5 cups)
3 ½ cups matzo farfel
1 (approximately 10 ½ ounces) can condensed clear chicken soup
1 cup water
1 teaspoon dried thyme
Salt and ground pepper to taste
3 large eggs or ¾ cup pareve egg substitute

1. Grease a 9 x 13 inch baking dish. Set aside.
2. Preheat oven to 350 degrees.
3. Put the oil into a 5-quart or larger pot and place over medium heat.
4. Add onion & garlic and sauté them until onion is soft.
5. Stir in mushrooms and sauté an additional minute or two.
6. Add farfel and stir just until it is mixed in well. Turn off heat.
7. Add chicken soup and water and stir to mix in evenly.
8. Season mixture with thyme, salt & pepper.
9. Beat eggs lightly and stir into the farfel mixture until completely combined.
10. Transfer mixture to the baking dish and smooth the top.
11. Bake uncovered at 350 degrees for 45 minutes or until the top is firm and dry.

Note: This kugle can be used as stuffing for a turkey or other poultry.

Latkes (pronounced: LOT-KISS)

Home fries? Nope? McDonald's hash browns? .....well almost—but better.

I loved these **before** I was born. Potato + Onion + Chicken fat (ok, leave out the chicken fat) = LOVE! Follow this classic recipe (Jane was strictly forbidden to modify this with threats of being disowned by the family) Fry-em up nice and crispy drain and serve. Wait till the pan cools before picking away at those munchy morsels left in the pan. Serve with sour cream or apple sauce. I liked them with apple sauce. I only ate sour cream with rye-bread ends......but that's another story.

Crisp Fried Potato Latkes

Chanukah
Stovetop
10 Servings

Shopping List:
- Matzo meal
- Potatoes or other vegetables

Ingredients

*2 ½ lb Potatoes (baking type such as Russet or Idaho) peeled
1 large onion finely chopped
3 large eggs, lightly beaten
1 teaspoon salt or to taste
⅛ teaspoon black pepper, fresh ground - to taste
¼ cup matzo meal or 2 tablespoon all-purpose flour

1. Shred or grate the potatoes alternately with the onion to keep the potatoes from darkening. (The size of the shreds is a matter of personal taste.) Coarse shreds produce lacier latkes with rough edges. Fine shreds or grated potatoes produce denser, smoother latkes.)
2. Squeeze the excess liquid from the potato and onion shreds.
3. Mix in the eggs, salt, pepper and matzo meal (or flour). Let the mixture rest for about 5 minutes so that the matzo meal can absorb some moisture. If the mixture still seems very wet, add a bit more matzo meal.
4. In a very large skillet, over medium-high heat, heat oil that is about ⅛"-¼" deep until it is very hot but not smoking.
5. To form each latke, use a large spoon to transfer some of the potato mixture to the oil; then flatten the mixture slightly with the back of a spoon. The latkes will be irregularly shaped. Continue making latkes until the skillet is full, leaving a little room between each one to turn. Fry the latkes until they are well browned on both sides and crisp around the edges.
6. Drain them well on paper towels. Repeat the process until all the latkes are fried. Serve the latkes as soon as possible for the best taste and texture.
7. Accompany the latkes with applesauce, sour cream, and/or yogurt, as desired.

*You can use other vegetables for your latkes... Zucchini, sweet potatoes, carrots, or a variety of veggies.

Jewish Holiday Vegetables

Elegant Vegetable Casserole (Rosh Hashanah)

Mushroom Ragout (Passover)

Pomegranate-Balsamic-Glazed Carrots (Chanukah or Passover)

Elegant Vegetable Casserole

Rosh Hashanah

Oven at 350 degrees

Serves 14

Ingredients For Parsnip Potatoes

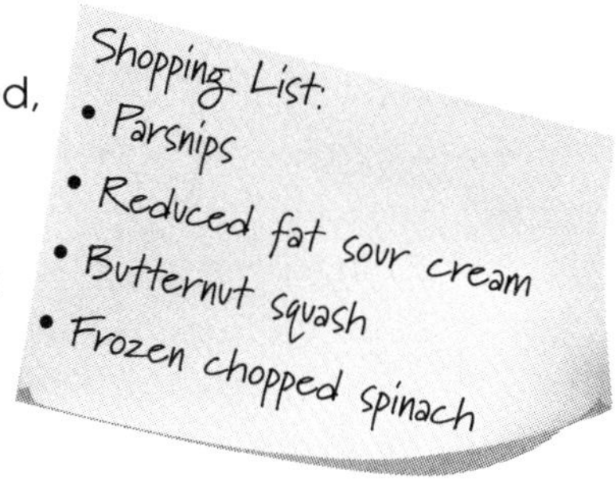

2 pounds potatoes (about 4 medium) peeled, & cubed

4 medium parsnips, peeled & cubed

1 carton (8 ounces) reduced fat sour cream

3 tablespoons fat-free milk

1 teaspoon salt

Ingredients For Squash

1 medium butter nut squash (about 3 pounds), peeled & cubed

½ teaspoon salt

¼ teaspoon ground nutmeg

Ingredients For Spinach

2 eggs

1 tablespoon fat-free milk

¼ teaspoon salt

2 packages (10 ounces each) frozen chopped spinach, thawed & squeezed dry

1 ½ cups (6 ounces) shredded reduced-fat Swiss cheese

¾ cup soft bread crumbs

1 small onion (grated)

1. Place potatoes & parsnips in a large saucepan and cover with water.
2. Bring to boil. Reduce heat, cover & simmer for 15 – 20 minutes or until tender.
3. Drain & mash with sour cream, milk & salt. Set aside.

4. Place squash in another large saucepan and cover with water.
5. Bring to boil. Reduce heat, cover & simmer for 15 – 20 minutes or until tender.
6. Drain & mash with salt & nutmeg. Set aside.
7. In a small bowl, whisk eggs, milk & salt. Stir in spinach, cheese, bread crumbs and onion.
8. Place half the parsnip potatoes at one end of a 13 – in x 9 in baking dish coated with cooking spray.
9. Add squash to dish forming a stripe.
10. Repeat with spinach
11. Place remaining parsnip potatoes at the opposite end of dish. (Dish will be full)
12. Cover & bake at 350 degrees or until meat thermometer inserted in the spinach reads 160 degrees.

Most special Jewish Holiday

I try hard NOT to be biased regarding Jewish Holidays. I did go to Hebrew school and I knew that Yom Kippur was the most special of special holidays. My Dad observed Yom Kippur; he observed that most Jewish people HE knew, tried to fast, tried to pray and didn't work. Pop really observed the latter. He unequivocally refused to work... unless Mamma had a dozen things for him to fix and, since that wasn't really work, work; he fixed what needed to be fixed.

I said, "Pop, won't God be mad at you? Won't you be punished? He said, "God will understand my boy....

I'll answer to God when I'm dead.....I answer to your Mamma now..."

OR

If God was married to your mother....even Yom Kippur, he'd be fixing things around the house.

Mushroom Ragout

Passover

Top of stove or electric fry pan

Serves 6 to 8

Ingredients

¼ cup olive oil

1 medium onion, chopped

1 pound mushrooms, quartered

½ teaspoon dried thyme (do not use ground. It is too strong)

1 teaspoon dried cumin seeds

½ teaspoon salt

½ teaspoon paprika

¼ teaspoon freshly ground pepper

Pinch of cayenne

2 tablespoons dry white wine

2 tablespoons chopped fresh parsley

1. Heat oil over medium heat in large skillet.
2. Add onions and sauté about 7 minutes until tender.
3. Add mushrooms, thyme, cumin, salt and pepper.
4. After 5 minutes, add wine.
5. Sauté stirring often for 10 – 15 additional minutes or until mushrooms are well coated with spices and any liquid has evaporated
6. Add cayenne, taste and adjust seasoning. Sprinkle with parsley.

Pomegranate-Balsamic-Glazed Carrots

Glazed carrots never had it so good. Bright, fresh flavors and a little cayenne play well with any rich main dish or holiday meal.

Stove top

Serves 8

Ingredients

Shopping List:
- Pomegranate juice
- Fresh mint

¼ cup pure pomegranate juice

1- 2 Tablespoons balsamic vinegar

4 teaspoons honey (to taste)

1 oz. (2 tablespoons) unsalted butter

2 Tablespoons extra-virgin olive oil

2 lb. carrots, trimmed, peeled, and cut into sticks about 2 inches long and 3/8 inch wide .

Kosher salt

⅓ cup lower-salt chicken broth

⅛ teaspoon cayenne

2 Tablespoons lightly packed thinly sliced fresh mint

1. Combine the juice, vinegar, and honey in a liquid measuring cup and whisk.
2. Cut 1 tablespoon of the butter into 4 pieces and refrigerate.
3. In a 12-inch skillet, heat the remaining 1 tablespoon butter with the olive oil over medium-high heat.
4. When the butter has melted, add the carrots and 1-½ teaspoons salt and toss well to coat. Cook without stirring until the bottom layer of carrots is lightly browned in spots, 4 to 5 minutes.
5. Flip the carrots and then leave undisturbed for 1 to 2 minutes to brown. Continue cooking, occasionally stirring and flipping, until most of the carrots are a bit browned in places and are starting to feel tender, an additional 3 to 5 minutes. Reduce the heat to medium if the bottom of the pan begins to brown too much.

6. Carefully add the chicken broth, cover quickly, and cook until all but about 1 tablespoon of the broth has evaporated, about 2 minutes.
7. Uncover, reduce the heat to medium low, and add the pomegranate mixture (re-whisk, if necessary) and the cayenne.
8. Cook, stirring gently, until the mixture reduces and becomes slightly glazy, about 1 minute.
9. Take the pan off the heat, add the chilled butter, and gently toss with a heatproof spatula until the butter has melted, 30 seconds to 1 minute.

Season to taste with salt and stir in about two-thirds of the mint. Serve in a warm shallow bowl or on a platter, garnished with the remaining mint.

The holiest day of the Jewish calendar is Yom Kippur except for the Sabbath—that's holier. The Sabbath is always holier unless Yom Kippur comes out on the Sabbath; then I'm not sure what happens. It's like that Y2K fiasco—the planets realign, Arabs start loving Jews, Skinheads accept all mankind?????

My Italian family, albeit half my family, always asked me... "I always forget....which is the happy Holiday, Yom Kippur or Rosh Hashanah?"

As a child, I knew Yom Kippur was the "sad" holiday and Rosh Hashanah was the "Happy" holiday. My reasoning? FOOD! There was none on Yom Kippur; there was tons on Rosh Hashanah. Case closed!

My Dad fasted on Yom Kippur but under the subliminal influence of Mamma, an overbearing Sicilian who could beat most men in an arm wrestle; Dad's fasting, and mine, were modified to better suit the needs of a "mixed" family.

On Yom Kippur, Daddy and I fasted between 12:01 midnight and Breakfast, from 9:00AM till lunch and then we both fasted till dinner—with the occasional in between snack just in case our respective blood sugars slipped below "above average." God forgives non-fasting for medicinal purposes.

Then, at nightfall, we have "break the fast" at my Aunt Ida's house—she was an Orthodox Jew who fasted .....till she blacked out.

Rosh Hashanah was quite different; it was like Christmas day at Aunt Millie's.

You ate....until you blacked out.

Jewish Holiday Desserts

Festival Strawberry Trifle (Chanukah)

Pear-Raspberry Tart
(Rosh Hashanah or "Break-the-fast" for Yom Kippur)

Soutlach (Creamy Rice Pudding)
(Shavuot or "Break-the-fast" for Yom Kipuer)

Festive Strawberry Trifle

This is a wonderfully delicious fresh strawberry trifle. Easy to make, and if you can get fresh strawberries where you live during the holiday season, I highly recommend making this for Hanukkah.

No cook

8 -10 servings

Ingredients

1 package lady fingers or chocolate pound cake, sliced into cubes

8 oz. cream cheese

16 oz. sour cream

1 package instant vanilla pudding

1 cup milk

¾ cup granulated sugar

2 pints fresh strawberries, washed and hulled, and cut in halves

¼ cup sliced almonds

2-3 cups whipped cream

Garnish

Approximately ½ dozen Whole Strawberries

Chocolate Curls

Mint Sprigs

1. Arrange a layer of lady fingers or chocolate pound cake cubes in the bottom of a large glass trifle bowl or other large glass bowl.
2. Whip the cream cheese and sour cream with sugar and add the pudding mixed with milk until you get a smooth mixture.
3. Divide into two and cover the lady fingers or chocolate pound cake cubes with half the quantity.

4. Decorate with strawberry halves and sliced almonds, and cover with whipped cream.
5. Repeat the arrangement of the layers, and top with whole strawberries and whipped cream.
6. Garnish trifle with chocolate curls and mint sprigs. Keep trifle refrigerated.

Pear-Raspberry Tart

Rosh Hashanah or Yom Kippur "break-fast"

Oven 375 degrees

Serves 6

Ingredients For Crust & Topping

1 ¼ cups all-purpose flour

1 cup quick rolled oats

⅓ cup granulated sugar

⅓ cup packed dark brown sugar

1 teaspoon baking power

¼ cup canola or vegetable oil

¼ cup water

½ teaspoon almond extract

Shopping List:
- Seedless raspberry preserves

Ingredients For Filling

1 large ripe pear (Bartlett or Anjou)

½ cup seedless raspberry preserves

1. Coat a 9-inch round tart or cake pan or an 8-inch square pan with non-stick cooking spray.
2. Preheat oven to 375 degrees.
3. Prepare crust & topping by putting flour, oats, granulated and brown sugars and baking powder into a medium bowl and mix with a fork to combine.
4. Add oil, water & almond extract and mix to make moist crumbs.
5. Remove 1 cup of the mixture and set aside.
6. Press the rest into the bottom of the prepared pan.
7. Peel, core and thinly slice the pear.
8. Spread the preserves on top of the crust.
9. Top with the pear.
10. Sprinkle the reserved crust mixture on top.
11. Bake at 375 degrees for about 35 minutes or until pear is tender and crust is firm.
12. Cool completely before cutting into wedges to serve.

Soutlach (Creamy Rice Pudding)

Shavuot or Yom Kippur "Break-the-fast" Breakfast
Top of Stove
Serves 6

Shopping List:
• Cream of Rice cereal

Ingredients

6 Tablespoons uncooked "Cream of Rice" cereal
⅓ cup sugar
4 cups milk, any type (I used 2% and it was terrific)
1 teaspoon vanilla extract
Ground cinnamon for sprinkling on top, to taste
Whipped cream (optional)

1. In a large saucepan, combine "Cream of Rice" cereal and sugar.
2. Slowly add the milk, stirring constantly so no lumps form.
3. Put saucepan over medium-high heat and cook, stirring constantly for 5 to 10 minutes (be careful that the cereal doesn't start to stick to the bottom & burn).
4. Cook until pudding begins to thicken and comes to a boil.
5. Lower heat so the pudding just simmers and cook, stirring often for 15 to 20 minutes. (The pudding should be thick and coat the spoon when you lift the spoon)
6. Remove from heat and stir in the vanilla.
7. Pour into 6 small bowls or one large shallow serving bowl.
8. Lightly sprinkle with cinnamon.
9. Serve the pudding warm or chilled.
10. Add whipped cream for a special treat.

BUT WAIT....THERE'S MORE!

FLIP THE COOKBOOK OVER TO FIND STEVE'S FAVORITE JEWISH & ITALIAN RECIPES AND MORE HILARIOUS STORIES ABOUT HIS WACKY FAMILY

BUT WAIT....THERE'S MORE!

FLIP THE COOKBOOK OVER TO FIND STEVE'S FAVORITE HOLIDAY RECIPES AND MORE HILARIOUS STORIES ABOUT HIS WACKY FAMILY